CU00657093

Table of Contents

*Photograph of the former Ramsey house utilized on the front cover was taken by Rick Pawlenty of St. Cloud, Minnesota

Disclaimer: The intent of this book was to review and analyze the circumstances surrounding the death of JonBenét Ramsey. None of my opinions or the presentation of case information should be construed as implying anyone is guilty or innocent in the death of JonBenét. The use of the word "suspect" does not imply someone was an official police suspect, but that the individual may have been or should have been closely reviewed regarding this case.

The conclusions drawn are not definitive, and they are based on likely outcomes rather than conclusive information. Many attempts were made to demonstrate the less than definitive nature of the information presented within this document. Wording such as, "most likely," "probably," etc. reflects the decision by the author to acknowledge deficiencies in the information around this investigation, though measures were taken to try to confirm or cross-check information.

There is little official and confirmed information regarding JonBenét's death and subsequent investigation. Much of the information gathered and theories presented is contended by those involved. Circumstances, evidence, and investigative actions identified in this book should <u>not</u> be considered facts

as they are based on second-hand, third-hand, or
even more detached sources. Even validated sources
have to be viewed skeptically, and the information
they presented should not be considered facts within
this book. All theories and extrapolations are my
opinions and should not be considered facts.

Foreword

The death of JonBenét Ramsey shocked and intrigued the nation, though I had no particular interest in it. I gave the case no additional thought until I read *The Cases that Haunt Us*, by John Douglas in 2010. *The Cases that Haunts Us* covered a handful of famous unsolved murders. Mr. Douglas attempted to apply a criminal profile system he developed to the unsolved cases. None of the crimes seemed to fit into his contrived categories, which resulted in some cases falling into several of the categories, thus eliminating the benefit of having categories. The reasoning behind the conclusion of one case contradicted the reasoning in another case.

Upon finishing the section on the JonBenét Ramsey murder in *The Cases that Haunts Us*, I was displeased with how the author arrived at his conclusions, and I felt it warranted greater research. I focused on finding all the information I could on the case. I wanted to read and analyze the data, as well as read every possible theory that had been floated. I also visited Boulder, Colorado to see the Ramsey house and neighborhood, as well as try to better understand the city and culture. I read almost every book ever written on this case, and in most instances I read the books multiple times. I studied interviews, television programs, and of course, the ransom note. Upon my initial review of the materials, I was not sure if Ramseys were guilty or innocent, but I was disgusted with their behavior. Specifically, I was bothered by John Ramsey, who was intelligent and successful, though he was completely incapable of doing or saying the right thing.

A late-term reading on my list was *The Death of Innocence* by John and Patsy Ramsey. I did not want to read it as I felt it would just be a longer, biased version of their television interviews, which conveyed deception, ignorance, and arrogance. To the contrary, I thought the book provided a good portrayal of what they went through after the murder of their daughter. The book provided their prospective, which was a needed contrast to most of what has been written about JonBenét's death. No matter what happened during the night of December 25, 1996, John and Patsy Ramsey had to cope with the loss of a child and the utter destruction the media thrust upon them.

Introduction

JonBenét Ramsey, a pretty six year-old girl, was found murdered in her home on December 26, 1996 in Boulder, Colorado. Her parents and older brother were home at the time. There were no signs of forced entry. Consequently, the police initially suspected the parents, John and Patsy Ramsey. When a child is murdered, crime statistics point overwhelmingly toward family members as the likely perpetrators. As a victim's age decreases, the more likely a family member was involved in the murder. The crime statistics point toward the parents, but statistics alone do not prove guilt. Further analysis is necessary.

The parents' behavior was consistent with the actions of guilty persons. On the morning of December 26, 1996, Patsy Ramsey visually stalked the arriving police officer through her fingers as he moved about the house. John and Patsy Ramsey remained distant throughout the morning. On scene victim advocates thought they were either separated or divorced. That afternoon, twenty minutes after John discovered JonBenét's dead body he made flight arrangements to leave the state. The Ramseys attempted to explain their actions and statements surrounding the death of their daughter, but their behaviors conveyed guilt.

Though the Ramsey's behavior was odd and guilt-ridden, it was excusable due to the stressful circumstances. The Ramseys were not thinking clearly during the time surrounding the death of JonBenét. Their daughter was dead, most likely murdered, and John initially suspected someone close to the family. The Ramseys were in the midst of the most stressful and overwhelming event of their lives.

The Ramsey's longer-term approach and actions to the murder investigation were well within their control; these actions were calculated. The Ramseys chose to not cooperate with the police. The Ramseys decided to go on television prior to talking to the police, even though their "excuse" for not talking to police was a combination of the media hype and Patsy's inability to function. Neither of these factors, however, prevented the Ramseys from going on national television. Engaging the public via a media outlet furthered the media frenzy around JonBenét's murder and most likely exacerbated Patsy's already weakened mental condition. The Ramseys tried to manipulate the media, and subsequently the public, all the while avoiding the police. Almost as disturbing as the Ramsey's failure to cooperate with the police was their strong desire and effort to convince everyone that they did cooperate.

A final element of the Ramsey's behavior was their deliberate and regular deception throughout the investigation. Every interview response and staged event reeked of inauthenticity. John and Patsy did not provide straight-forward answers. The police investigating the murder immediately identified the inconsistencies and evasion in the Ramsey's statements and behavior.

The strange circumstances of the murder, coupled with the Ramsey's behavior placed considerable suspicion upon them. The Ramsey's public relations campaign and refusal to talk to the police further enhanced this perception. At the same time, the Ramseys portrayed themselves as victims. Not victims because they were parents of a murdered child, but victims of the media. The Ramseys were victims of a biased Boulder Police Department and a narrow-minded District Attorney's Office. They were victims of a powerful media campaign against them. With all the money spent and resources devoted, the Ramseys still could not shape public opinion in their favor. The Ramsey's focus on their reputation and self-interest will forever tarnish any respect they hope to reclaim.

Understanding, and potentially solving, this case is about seeking justice for the murder of an innocent girl. It is not about keeping John and Patsy Ramsey out of prison at the expense of justice for JonBenét. Moral persons sacrifice their freedom to protect and seek justice for those they love. The search for the truth must move forward, regardless of where it may lead.

The vicious murder and molestation of JonBenét Ramsey drew national and international attention. JonBenét, the daughter of wealthy, attractive, and successful parents, was the first murder of 1996 in the small city of Boulder, Colorado. On Christmas night while her parents slept, a girl from an upper-middle class family was taken from her bed in the middle of the night. The beauty and innocence of JonBenét contrasted sharply with the brutality and horror of the events that unfolded after she was taken from her bedroom.

As more information flowed out of the investigation, the more coverage the murder received. The potential involvement of the parents in the murder drove interest in the crime exponentially. John and

Patsy Ramsey appeared ordinary. There were no apparent vices or unusual behaviors in their past other than the child beauty pageants; a topic completely unrelated to the crime, but a regular fixation of the press. There was no motive for murder. Notwithstanding, the parents immediately retained lawyers and refused to cooperate with the police.

When the Ramseys refused to talk with the police, people were outraged. The parents had an obligation to help find the killer of their child, regardless of what the police thought. Many believed only a guilty parent would not assist the police in the murder investigation of their child.

Besides the lack of cooperation by the Ramseys, they also exhibited clear and consistent behaviors indicative of deception. Law enforcement took notice of the Ramsey's questionable behavior. It was also one of the reasons why most of the assigned investigators to the JonBenét case initially believed the Ramseys were involved. Throughout the investigation and during television interviews, the Ramseys routinely misled, deceived, and manipulated answers for various reasons. Some of the deception was direct and obvious, while others required context or a literal interpretation of the question or answer. Some Ramsey comments may have been mistakes or failure of memory, but in most cases the deception was deliberate. Seemingly normal parents put their self-interest ahead of justice for their daughter. John and Patsy Ramsey hid behind the banner of legality while ignoring morality.

John and Patsy Ramsey retained legal representation within days of JonBenét's murder. It was their legal right, but it did not move the investigation forward. It is understandable that the parents wanted to know their legal rights, but it is another level to use lawyers to block the investigator's access to the only persons alive in the house the night of JonBenét's murder. Had any other witness or suspect in the investigation acted in the same manner as the Ramseys, he/she would still be under the "umbrella of suspicion."

One of the most important aspects of an interview is the gut feeling the interviewer derives from the interviewee. Many of these feelings are on a subconscious level, even to trained interviewers/interrogators. Though, the more training and experience one receives, the more gut feelings can be turned into articulable statements. Is the person overly nervous? Is he evasive or deceptive? Are there chronological gaps? Does one part of the story have less detail than the rest of the statement?

An often misleading aspect of interviewing is when the interviewee is lying or showing deception for reasons other than the crime at hand. This may result in the investigator suspecting the individual of wrong-doing. For example, during the initial interview of U.S. Representative Gary Condit regarding the murder of Chandra Levy, Mr. Condit did not tell the authorities about his sexual relationship with Ms. Levy. He was married. He had something to hide. Most likely, the investigators picked up on the deception and uneasiness of Mr. Condit during the interview. As a result, the authorities started to direct their attention toward him as a possible suspect in the then disappearance of Chandra Levy.

Mr. Condit vehemently protected the discovery of his secret relationship with Ms. Levy, not because of his involvement in her murder, but because he was married. Acknowledging the relationship would have adversely impacted his marriage and career. Mr. Condit probably showed many signs of guilt. If he had not later come forward and cleared the air with the police, the authorities would have continued to suspect him. Mr. Condit's desire to withhold, what he probably viewed as irrelevant information to the investigation, resulted in the police diverting resources away from other leads. Finally, he corrected his early statements and allowed the police to focus on other avenues.

Ms. Levy's family told police they believed Mr. Condit was being evasive regarding their daughter. He avoided answering direct questions from the media, which furthered the perception of his involvement in the disappearance of Chandra Levy. Though Mr. Condit had nothing to do with the murder, his behavior cast suspicion over him throughout the investigation.

Another example of misdirected deception involved the notorious Saddam Hussein, the former President of Iraq. There was concern within the United States government and around the world that Iraq possessed nuclear weapons. Prior to the second Iraq war in 2003, nearly everyone believed Saddam was lying about having weapons of mass destruction ("WMD"). Though Iraq possessed biological and chemical weapons, concern focused on Iraq's possession and capabilities regarding a nuclear weapon.

Saddam refused to allow the United Nations' weapons inspectors into Iraq. When he finally allowed the weapons inspectors to search for WMD's, he placed stringent conditions around when, how, and where they could inspect. Throughout the process, Saddam claimed to be cooperating fully with the authorities. The question was posed, why would he lie about having WMD's? Why would Saddam risk war and most likely complete destruction of his country if he did not have WMD's? Therefore, he must have them.

In the end, at least according to a disgraced, weakened Saddam, he lied to prevent Iran from understanding the limited capabilities of Iraq's WMD. Cultural components played into Saddam's deception, but he wanted to deceive Iran, not the United States. Saddam was willing to risk utter destruction and death in order to maintain honor.

Prior to the 2008 presidential election, some right-wing activist groups and private citizens questioned Barrack Obama's United States' citizenship. After the election, the speculation continued. Various entities and individuals filed in court trying to compel President Obama to verify his citizenship by providing a certified birth certificate. Many defenders of the President thought the accusation was ridiculous and not worth a response. Yet, the President actively fought the lawsuits that were trying to compel him to provide a birth certificate. The government utilized numerous resources to defend the President.

President Obama's response to the controversy only increased the speculation. The President had his staff put a lessor form statement of birth on the White House website. It provided the same information as a birth certificate, but it was not considered a "birth certificate." The governor of Hawaii fought unsuccessfully to get the President's birth certificate released. Afterward, a state of Hawaii official viewed the birth certificate. He subsequently signed a statement indicating the authenticity of the birth certificate and verified Barrack Obama was born in Hawaii (United States).

The President's failure to release his birth certificate and his dismissive responses to reporter questions fueled the controversy and resulted in a variety of theories surrounding its true contents. People speculated his birth certificate stated he was Muslim, or it was somehow personally embarrassing. If the President was not a United States' citizen, the repercussions were almost unimaginable.

In the end, a quasi-serious presidential contender with a checkered past named Donald Trump forced the President to provide his birth certificate. It proved that the President was born in America, and there were no damaging items on his birth certificate. What prevented the President from turning over his birth certificate? Most likely, it was nothing more than ego. The President chose to waste tax payer dollars fighting lawsuits rather than turn over his birth certificate, simply because he did not want to provide it.

The three examples listed above are all politicians. Not surprisingly, in recent years, John Ramsey ran (and lost) for public office. John Ramsey demonstrated a tremendous ego throughout the investigation of his daughter's murder. John regularly placed his ego above helping find the killer(s) of his daughter.

John and Patsy Ramsey expressed extensive, blatant, and consistent indicators of deception. This led law enforcement to believe one or both of the Ramseys were involved in the death of JonBenét. Similar to the stories illustrated above, there was a possibility the Ramseys were showing signs of deception for reasons other than their involvement in the murder of

JonBenét or in addition to their involvement. One cannot immediately equate deception with guilt.

John and Patsy Ramsey's motives can be understood by analyzing their actions, words, and behaviors. Identifying and analyzing the Ramsey's deceptive and often confusing behaviors, coupled with probable outcomes and conjecture will unwind the likely events surrounding the death of JonBenét. The Ramsey's actions did not fit with conventional wisdom or logic. Therefore, logic (or lack of) as a reasoning for explaining the Ramsey's action or inaction is not a definitive basis for making assumptions about what occurred.

Absent a signed confession accompanied by supporting circumstantial evidence, it is unlikely there will ever be a criminal conviction or even closure in this case. The flawed police work, accompanied by an incompetent District Attorney's Office will prevent a conviction. The management of this investigation has allowed and promoted an environment where "reasonable doubt" will always be present.

Chapter 1 – "Something isn't right"

For the Ramseys, Christmas morning 1996 unfolded in typical fashion. The Ramseys rose early to open presents and celebrate the holiday. A late breakfast followed the opening of gifts. After breakfast, the children played with toys while Patsy engaged in various house-related activities. John left the house during the afternoon to check on his plane in preparation for the family's trip to Michigan. The family planned to leave early the next morning to visit their lake home and meet other family members. Late in the afternoon of December 25th, the Ramsey family (John, Patsy, Burke, and JonBenét) drove to Fleet and Priscilla White's house for a holiday gathering. They arrived around 4:00 p.m. The adults ate, drank, and conversed while the children played and ate. No one reported any unusual or noteworthy events or activities from the holiday party.

Numerous sources provided varying estimates on the time the Ramseys left the White's party, but most accounts place their departure between 8:30 p.m. and 9:00 p.m. During the short trip home, the Ramseys made two stops on the way. The Ramseys dropped off gifts at Stewart and Roxy Walker's and Glenn and Susan Stine's houses. Patsy got out of the car and took the gifts to the Walkers, while she and Burke (JonBenét's nine year-old brother) presented gifts to the Stines. The family arrived home sometime between 9:00 p.m. and 9:30 p.m.

According to John and Patsy's two official interviews (the Ramseys were interviewed by the Boulder Police Department in April of 1997 and the Boulder District Attorney's Office in June of 1998), JonBenét fell asleep in the car during the ride home, and she never awoke during the arrival home and subsequent preparation for bed. John carried JonBenét from the car to bed while Patsy helped Burke into the house. On December 26th, John told three police officers, separately, he read to the "children" when they got home the previous night. In the April 1997 interviews, John stated the officers inaccurately recorded events from the 25th, and the officers most likely misunderstood him. According to Burke Ramsey's interview statement, JonBenét was awake when the family arrived home on the night of the 25th, and she walked slowly up the spiral staircase behind Patsy.

If John and Patsy misled investigators regarding JonBenét being asleep during the arrival home, it is not clear what potential purpose it would it serve, other than establish a more definitive time for when

JonBenét was asleep. Since John and Patsy were asked about the circumstances of the arrival home, both in official interviews and on television programs, their answers should be taken as their recollections of the transpired events. The Ramseys committed to JonBenét being asleep upon their arrival home, thus mitigating speculation JonBenét could have been playing with Burke or awake later than her parents. If she was awake with Burke in the late hours of December 25th then Burke's testimony about the night's events would have become more critical. As a result, the Ramsey's statements regarding their arrival home reduced Burke's potential involvement in the investigation.

Once in her bedroom, John laid JonBenét on her bed, but Patsy dressed her for bed. Patsy replaced JonBenét's black pants with long underwear pants. To avoid waking her, Patsy chose to leave on her white shirt with a rhinestone sequence star. In early accounts, Patsy stated she put JonBenét to bed in a red turtleneck, which was found balled up on JonBenét's bathroom counter. At no other time did she reiterate that statement. While Patsy attended to JonBenét, John helped Burke assemble a toy he got for Christmas. At some point after their arrival home, Patsy placed presents by the back door. John and Patsy retreated to their third floor bedroom about

10:00 p.m. They fell asleep around 10:30 p.m. No one in the house claimed to have heard anything unusual during the night.

On December 26th, John stated he awoke before the alarm, around 5:25 a.m. He proceeded to take a shower and get ready for the day. Patsy was still in asleep when John got out of bed. According to Patsy, she awoke by the alarm at 5:30 a.m. She put on her make-up, got dressed, and headed downstairs to pack some last minute items and make coffee.

Considerable attention was given to Patsy wearing the same clothes on the morning of December 26th as she wore the previous night. Many investigators believed Patsy had stayed up all night; hence, the reason why she wore the same clothes the following day. As a former beauty queen, Patsy conveyed an image overly concerned with appearance. On the morning of December 26th, she put on make-up and did her hair, but she wore the same clothes from the previous night. When asked about this, Patsy stated she regularly wore the same clothes two days in a row. Just to reinforce the point, Patsy wore the same clothes the day after the interview as she did during the interview when investigators confronted her about wearing the same clothes two days in a row. This stunt did not sit well with the police as it looked like another deceptive tactic by the Ramseys. However, based on statements by John, Patsy was in bed when he awoke, thus she had to have gone to bed at some point during the night. This statement may have been a cover by John, but there is no indication of this.

After Patsy left the third floor, she stated she stopped on the second floor, outside of JonBenét's room, to take some last minute clothes from the dryer and place them into a garbage bag for the Michigan trip they were to take that day. She then proceeded down the back, spiral staircase to the first floor where she found one of the most crucial pieces of evidence, the ransom note. During this timeframe, John and Patsy's statements varied considerably and contradicted each other.

Based on the time Patsy awoke and the timing of the 9-1-1 call, she headed down the back spiral staircase sometime around 5:45 a.m. As Patsy walked down the spiral staircase, she saw three papers spread across a step near the bottom. She stepped over the note and turned to look at it. According to Lawrence Schiller in *Perfect Murder Perfect Town*, the Boulder Police Department tried to replicate Patsy's claimed movements on the steps, but they were unable to complete them. The police could not step over three pieces of paper laid across one of the lower stair rungs without falling (Schiller 1999). The failure to replicate Patsy's stated actions somewhat discredits her recollection of those events.

Patsy claimed she read the ransom note up to where it said, "…we have your daughter…" At this point, Patsy claimed she ran back up the spiral staircase to check on JonBenét. She pushed open the door, and without entering the room, saw JonBenét was not in her bed. In a state of panic, she screamed for John!

During initial discussions with police on December 26th, Patsy indicated she looked into JonBenét's room, observed she was not there, and then descended the back stairs. In all subsequent interviews and statements, Patsy contended she did not look into JonBenét's room prior to finding the note. By extrapolating from the numerous different versions presented by both Ramseys, Patsy yelled for John prior to ascending the spiral staircase after finding the ransom note. As a result, Patsy had either already looked in JonBenét's room and knew she was not there, or she called out for John prior to even checking her daughter's room.

If this was the case, the only evidence she had of JonBenét's absence was the ransom note. She had only read a couple of lines. Almost anyone in this situation would be in denial. She would have not taken a hand-written note as proof her daughter had been taken. A horrific thought to any parent and one she would most likely not accept so quickly. Another possibility is that Patsy changed her story for some reason, and her initial explanation of looking into JonBenét's bedroom prior to going downstairs was correct. Therefore, she already knew JonBenét was not in her room.

When Patsy screamed, John was on the third floor getting ready for the day. According to Patsy's description of events, she was standing just outside JonBenét's bedroom on the second floor when she yelled for John. *The location from where Patsy supposedly screamed was very close to the location where JonBenét may have been abducted.* In John Ramsey's April 1997 interviews, he stated once he heard Patsy's scream he immediately ran down the stairs. John stated Patsy was running up the stairs as he was running down the stairs. They met on the second floor. Patsy should have already been on the second floor because she screamed *after* she looked into JonBenét's room. She would not have been running up the stairs to the second floor at the same time John was running down the stairs. If Patsy remained on the first floor or lower part of the spiral staircase (where she found the ransom note) when she yelled for John, then Patsy's official statements were not correct.

In Patsy's first statement to the police on the morning of December 26th, she indicated she looked in JonBenét's room prior to walking down the stairs. Is this the true account of what happened? If so, it would begin to explain why Patsy did not need to look in JonBenét's room to know she was gone. If her official recollection of the events is correct then somehow Patsy knew JonBenét had been taken without even looking in the child's bedroom. Patsy's response to reading a few lines of a hand-written note were not what one would expect. Denial would be expected. A likely reaction would have been for Patsy to run around the house looking and screaming for JonBenét. Instead, she immediately believed the contents of the note.

Most of John Ramsey's statements throughout both official interviews and during television interviews were precise and confident. In contrast, John's statements surrounding the time he responded to Patsy's screams were not. One could argue his recollection was affected by extreme stress; however, John provided specific and confident details regarding when he found his daughter's dead body.

After Patsy called for him, John was unclear on how things occurred during this timeframe. He may have been withholding information, or he may have changed his story and is not able to keep it straight. During John's April 1997 interviews, he stated Patsy handed him the note after he "intercepted her" on the second floor. Then he stated the note was on the first floor. John further stated, "Patsy was either coming up the stairs or was fully up [when he met her]." In John's June 1998 interviews, he stated Patsy handed him the note on the second floor. John statements surrounding his first contact with the ransom note were not clear or consistent.

Patsy stated she told John "They" have JonBenét and then she handed him the note. During Patsy's June 1998 official interviews, she was not sure if she handed John the note or if it was on the first floor. During the same interview, Patsy stated, "But I know I left the note…" She also indicated John asked where the note was when they spoke on the second floor. As with John's statements, Patsy does not provide a firm explanation of the ransom note's location during her first encounter with John that morning.

Patsy did not remember if she had the note with her or not. Patsy held to her story of meeting John on the second floor, but this portion of the timeline caused her to question where the note was or should have been during this episode; and hence (reference to the ransom note intended), she did not want to state with any conviction where the note was during this time.

Though the Ramseys were vague and contradictory in their statements surrounding the finding of the ransom note, in their book *The Death of Innocence*, they put it down in writing. According to the Ramsey's book, Patsy did not have the note with her when she met John on the second floor landing. Patsy told John the ransom note was on the first floor. He then ran down the stairs to get the note. He yelled to Patsy asking about Burke's safety. At this point, they both checked on Burke. They determined he was okay and that it was best to leave him sleeping. After checking on Burke, John ran down the main stairs and into the back hallway where he read the note while kneeling on the floor (Ramsey 2001). *After making this statement in the book, it is not clear whether or not the Ramseys went back to the Boulder Police Department to ensure they had the correct chronology of events on the morning of December 26th, or they just expected the police to read the book and adjust their information as necessary.*

After the discovery of the ransom note, John and Patsy were not clear on the progression of events. Though neither John nor Patsy could pinpoint when exactly they checked on Burke, based on their various interviews and Burke's recollection both parents checked on Burke during the early morning hours. At this time, both parents presumably thought JonBenét had been kidnapped. Burke's safety would become a paramount concern for John and Patsy. Yet, according to the interviews, neither parent did anything more than observe Burke sleeping. Neither parent verified Burke was not harmed nor did they keep him with them. There was no reason for John and Patsy to believe the "intruders" were gone. The ransom note implied the intruders left the house with JonBenét; however, it was possible that they could still be in the house. John and Pasty were not fearful for their safety or for Burke's during the early morning hours of December 26th.

Patsy dialed 9-1-1 at 5:52 a.m., while John read the ransom note kneeling on the floor in his underwear. John placed himself in a completely vulnerable position given the fact a stranger had just broken into the house. He left himself open and defenseless against a potential attack by an intruder. He showed no concern for his safety. John was either in shock, or he was starting to piece things together, thus he realized there may not have been an intruder. After the 9-1-1 call, John indicated he "…looked around a little more." According to the Ramsey's book, John looked under JonBenét's bed. He did not mention searching any other areas of the house other than a walk-in refrigerator, nor did he pick up a weapon while searching the house. No one really looked for JonBenét. A ransom note was found and both parents automatically believed that their daughter had been taken.

John went upstairs to get dressed. Though he was clearly not in the proper state of mind, it is not reasonable for John to waste time putting on slacks and a button-down shirt when he has not thoroughly checked the house for JonBenét or an intruder. Prior to the police arriving, Patsy was on the first floor, Burke was on the second floor, and John was on the third floor. Everyone was in a separate part of the house with no measures taken to protect or safeguard the family members.

After calling 9-1-1, Patsy called John and Barbara Fernie, followed by Fleet and Priscilla White. In a panic she asked the two couples to come over to the house. Reverend Hoverstock also arrived later in the morning. As a result, the Fernies, Whites, and

Reverend Hoverstock were all in the house with John and Patsy Ramsey during the morning. After making the calls, Patsy stayed on the first floor pacing and praying.

Officer French of the Boulder Police Department arrived around 6:00 a.m. on the morning of December 26th. Officer French described the actions of the parents as very unusual. Patsy Ramsey watched Officer French through her fingers as she covered her face while crying. She followed his every action as he moved about the house. At one point during the day, Officer French said to another police officer, "something isn't right." Many of Officer French's statements were only suspicions or gut feelings, not reaching the level of articulable facts. Though, it does not mean what he observed was inaccurate. Many of the Ramsey's actions were not consistent with the circumstances and warranted additional inquiries.

John told Officer French, Detective Arndt, and Sergeant Whitson that he checked the house before going to bed the previous night, and it was locked and secure. John had these three discussions independently of each other. John would later try to recant and mitigate the statements he made regarding the security status of the house prior to JonBenét's murder. Based on the police officers' observations, there were no signs of forced entry.

For the next several hours, dozens of persons entered and exited the house. Family friends roamed the house freely. The police did not officially seal off JonBenét's bedroom until 10:30 a.m. As time passed and there was no ransom call, police officers started to leave the Ramsey house. As noon approached, Detective Linda Arndt was the only police officer in the house. Due to the lack of police support and the number of family and friends in the house, she was concerned that she was losing control of the situation. In reality, the situation at the crime scene had been out of control for hours. The lack of police personnel during this timeframe resulted in further contamination of the evidence in the house.

Detective Arndt was unable to keep tabs on everyone's whereabouts. During the morning, she lost track of John Ramsey and thought he left the house. According to John, during the morning he went to the basement to look at the broken window in the train room. This may or may not have been the same time Detective Arndt lost track of him. No one knew John went to the basement; he divulged this information without prompting. There has been much speculation regarding what John did during his trip to the basement. Most of the theories are tied to Detective Arndt's assessment that John appeared more sullen after she lost track of him, which could have been due to any number of factors.

Around 1:00 p.m., in an attempt to occupy John Ramsey, Detective Arndt asked him to go through the house and document anything out-of-place or suspicious. Unfortunately, this decision resulted in irreparable harm to the crime scene and the evidence collection process. Since Fleet White was standing nearby, Detective Arndt asked him to accompany John on his search of the house. Fleet followed John to the basement where they inspected the broken window in the train room. John later indicated he wanted to see if there was enough glass on the floor to indicate a new break in the window. There was not. John told Fleet he broke the window the previous summer. During John's official interviews in April of 1997, he indicated the open window [in the basement] was not note-worthy because sometimes it was opened to let out heat. Later in the investigation, John completely changed his opinion and theories around the window. To him, it became evidence of an intruder.

After inspecting the window, John headed into the boiler room and to a back part of the basement where he unlatched the door to the wine cellar. Upon opening the door to the wine cellar, John indicated that he immediately saw JonBenét lying on the floor. Though John could not specifically recall whether the light was on or not, his statements implied he saw JonBenét prior to turning on the light in the wine cellar. Fleet was behind John as he entered the wine cellar. He also believed John saw JonBenét prior to turning on the light.

Fleet White had opened the same door during an earlier search of the house. He was unable to find the light switch so he did not enter. Fleet stood at approximately the same location as John when he saw the white blanket wrapped around JonBenét. Detectives placed significant emphasis on this apparent discrepancy. The theory, most widely circulated by Boulder Police Detective Steve Thomas, was that John discovered his daughter on the earlier trip to the basement. There is no direct evidence of this other than a perceived change in John's demeanor after his trip to the basement. At the time, however, the police did not know John previously went to the basement or what time he was down there. It was almost pure conjuncture for the police to try to line up John's supposed change in demeanor with a visit to the basement.

When Fleet entered the room earlier in the morning, he was looking for a light switch. Most likely, he would have been looking around the room, specifically at the walls, slightly above waist level. He may not have even looked toward the floor. John Ramsey said he saw the "white blanket," which he knew was JonBenét's, hence, why he thought she was in the room. He did not initially see JonBenét lying on the floor. If Fleet had seen the blanket, he would not have identified it as relating to JonBenét. Therefore, John identifying something Fleet White was unable to see does not mean anything questionable or unusual occurred.

Immediately upon opening the door to the wine cellar, John saw a white blanket. John rushed into the room as he saw JonBenét lying on the cellar floor wrapped in a white blanket next to a pink nightgown. JonBenét was found at approximately 1:05 p.m. John tore off a piece of duct tape covering her mouth and tried to loosen the rope around her right wrist. The rope around JonBenét's wrist was later found to be loose, most likely due to John's attempts to remove the rope.

Fleet reached down and felt JonBenét's cold body. He ran upstairs yelling for someone to call 9-1-1, though John did not recall hearing Fleet say anything during this time. John Ramsey lifted her body and ran to the main floor of the house. John laid her on the floor near the front door. Detective Arndt picked up JonBenét and carried her into the living room. She placed her body on a rug in front of the Christmas tree. As Detective Arndt leaned over JonBenét, she pronounced her dead. Under his breath, John Ramsey uttered, "It had to be an inside job."

Patsy Ramsey entered the room shortly thereafter. She fell to the floor and hugged her daughter, praying and crying for Jesus to raise her child from the dead. John then placed a blanket over JonBenét. Detective Arndt moved the blanket so it only covered her body. Shortly afterward, someone placed a sweatshirt over JonBenét's exposed feet. Within minutes of the discovery of JonBenét, her body had been moved twice, touched by at least four people (John Ramsey, Fleet White, Detective Arndt, and Patsy Ramsey), and covered by two separate garments. Distinguishing what items and fibers related to the murder and what was due to the handling after JonBenét's body was found has still not been resolved. Within minutes of the discovery of JonBenét, the integrity of her body, forensically speaking, was compromised.

About twenty minutes after finding JonBenét dead, John Ramsey made a call to arrange for a private flight to Atlanta. The police did not view John's attempt to immediately leave Boulder, Colorado after the murder of his daughter well (Gentile 2003). John later explained he made the call because he feared for the safety of his family. This is a drastic shift from his behavior earlier in the morning. John and Patsy left Burke alone in his bed for over an hour after they found the ransom note. John placed himself on all fours on the floor while reading the note. John never conducted a thorough search of the house during the morning of December 26th. None of these actions indicate someone who was fearful for himself or his family.

During the morning of December 26th, John Ramsey later claimed to have observed many suspicious items, but he failed to alert the police inside his house. John claimed he saw a strange vehicle in the alley behind his neighbor's house, the Barnhills. He did not identify what made it strange, and he did not notify the authorities of this observation until his interviews in June of 1998, 18 months after the fact. John also stated a caller hung up during the morning, but according to Detective Steve Thomas, there was no recording of such call. Furthermore, John later indicated, in a misleading manner, he noticed an opened window in the basement with broken glass below it.

On December 26th, neither John nor Patsy were feeling persecuted by the police and had no reason to not raise concerns or suspicions. Most likely, John did not have any of these revelations until many months later. He was not in the right frame of mind, and most of his statements on that day indicated he was not aware of any indication of an intruder. Since the Ramseys were not immediately formally interviewed following the murder of their daughter, there was limited documentation pertaining to John's statements. To further complicate things, some of the police officers did not properly record statements made by John. Many other police observations were not properly documented as well. After the suspicion shifted to the Ramseys, his "memory" of the day's events became much clearer and more focused on items indicating the presence of one or more intruders.

Chapter 2 – The Players

Every major news story has a cast of characters. The circus surrounding the death of JonBenét was no different. The various players in the investigation and aftermath resided mainly in the Boulder, Colorado area. And on the world stage, Boulder did not receive good marks in professionalism or ethics. It was a race to the bottom among most of the participants: Boulder Police Department, Boulder District Attorney's Office, Federal Bureau of Investigation, Ramseys and legal team, and media.

Boulder Police Department

Theoretically, investigators and other law enforcement officials working a criminal investigation should exercise objectivity. No one should have a vested interest in one outcome over and another. Professionalism should override emotion and personal feelings. Of course, this is an idealistic view. People make work personal. With the increasing use of technology, many people are continuously linked to work, thus further graying the line between personal and professional time. At some level, personalizing work helps to justify time away from family and/or low pay. It adds value, beyond compensation, to what many spend most of their lives doing.

At least initially, the police investigating the murder of JonBenét were objective. However, the Boulder Police Department inexperience and unpreparedness to handle a high-profile child murder began to dilute their objectivity. In Boulder, community policing had replaced law enforcement. It is not surprising that a community fixated on protecting the wildlife and recycling would not be overly concerned with locking up criminals. Boulder prides itself at being different and its fifteen minutes of fame certainly depicted such. The liberal underpinnings of Boulder provided a basis for how many of the decisions surrounding the investigation was made.

On December 23, 1996 at 6:47 p.m. a 9-1-1 call was placed from the Ramsey residence in Boulder, Colorado. A police dispatcher answered the call, but the caller hung up without saying anything. The police called the number back only to get the answering machine. The police dispatched an officer to the house to investigate the call. He arrived at the house at 6:54 p.m. Through the intercom system, a person in the house, later reported to be a family friend, Susan Stine, assured the police officer no emergency existed. The officer made no additional inquiries and left the house at 7:09 p.m.

It is not evident how the officer ensured there was no emergency other than the word of the person with whom he spoke. At the time of the call, there was a Christmas party in the house and anyone could have accidently dialed 9-1-1. Some reports indicate Fleet White accidently made the call. Did the Boulder Police Department have procedures for handling 9-1-1 calls? Did the officer breach procedure by not entering the house or not? Either way, the officer determined nothing unseemly was going on in the residence. In hindsight, this was one of many signs of a complacent police organization.

Three days later another emergency call came from the Ramsey residence. This time, the call was not by accident. However, much of the police response to this call was no more inquisitive or skeptical than the previous response. The police did not treat the Ramsey house as a crime scene thus compromising the integrity of the evidence contained within.

The police department allowed the crime scene to be completely contaminated. Key pieces of evidence were forever tarnished as a result of decisions and indecision on the part of the Boulder Police. The failure to formally interview the Ramseys on December 26th ended any opportunity to get an unrehearsed explanation of what happened the previous night. For all the mistakes made by individual officers, the police leadership was ultimately responsible for the lack of preparation and training on the part of the police department.

Once the blatant mistakes were made and known to the public, there was plenty of blame to go around. Various members of the police department started to take the case personally. Emotion became a dominant factor to an organization that should have had no bias and only one goal: enforcing the law. As a result, some members of the police department leaked information about the case to the media. The individuals broached an ethical code they swore to uphold and significantly damaged the ongoing investigation. In the end, their hearts may have been in the right place, but the means they chose to reach their ends materially impaired their credibility.

Boulder District Attorney's Office

It is not clear what went wrong with the Boulder District Attorney's Office ("DA") during the JonBenét Ramsey murder investigation: incompetence, lack of experience, conflicts of interest, pursuit of fame, or some combination thereof. The DA's Office criticized the Boulder Police Department's handling of the case. Many of the attorneys within the DA's Office did not respect the police officers and detectives working the Ramsey investigation. The DA's Office also made many questionable decisions regarding subpoenas and other legal approaches when dealing with the Ramseys. The combination resulted in a very contentious relationship between the police and prosecuting attorneys. There was a complete lack of trust between the parties, and their inability to work together materially impacted the JonBenét murder investigation.

On several occasions, Deputy District Attorney Trip Demuth asked to have police reports changed if he did not like the content. The DA's Office refused to subpoena Ramsey phone records and credit card statements. The DA's Office denied numerous affidavits for search warrants submitted by the police. Consequently, case detectives spent countless hours manually searching for Ramsey receipts and conducting additional interviews to try to find information, which should have come from requested searches and subpoenaed information. In the end, the Boulder DA's Office utilized a grand jury to subpoena many of the same documents the

Office had already denied when the police had requested them. The DA wasted years with a strategy of informally asking the Ramseys for information rather than utilizing legal measures. Most requests for information were received with affirmative responses from the Ramsey legal team, but in many instances the information never reached the police. If the DA's Office had used legal channels, there would have been assurances the information was provided, and in a timely fashion.

Many within the DA's Office shared confidential information with Ramsey attorneys throughout the investigation. Specifically, Deputy District Attorney Pete Hofstrom asked Boulder detectives for updated information because the Ramsey legal team needed it to respond to newspaper reports. It has also been reported the DA's Office asked Hal Haddon, head of the Ramsey defense team, for advice during the investigation.

After the medical examiner completed JonBenét's autopsy, the Ramseys requested the release of the body for burial. The police needed to extract all physical evidence from her remains prior to burial. If anything was overlooked with regard to her body, it was unlikely they would exhume the body for additional testing. The police had to obtain all the information they needed prior to turning the body over to the parents. It is not clear whether Commander John Eller tried to use JonBenét's body as leverage to get the parents to cooperate or not. Regardless, Deputy DA Pete Hofstrom told Commander Eller he could not "ransom the body!" Interestingly, the media reported the exact same phrase almost contemporaneously. This is one of numerous instances where the DA's Office in Boulder showed a lack of professionalism and an inability maintain confidences.

In early 1997, the Boulder DA's Office hired Mr. Lou Smit to assist with the Ramsey investigation. Lou Smit was a retired police detective who worked over one hundred and fifty murder investigations. His experience with homicide investigations probably outweighed the entire Boulder Police Department. Mr. Smit acted as a devil's advocate to the path the Boulder Police Department was taking regarding the guilt of the Ramseys. He punched holes in their case, as a defense team would try to do. Coming into this case, Mr. Smit's investigative skills were highly respected.

Originally, Mr. Smit exhibited skepticism toward the Ramsey's innocence, but he quickly changed his mind. Mr. Smit is considered the father of the "intruder theory." He believed there was clear and convincing evidence an intruder invaded the Ramsey house and killed JonBenét. He cited a boot print, a suitcase under the basement window, and leaves from the window sill in the basement, among other items as proof of an intruder. Further, Mr. Smit did not think the Ramseys killed their daughter based on unofficial discussions he had with them.

Mr. Smit provided a strong and initially objective opinion to counter the police who seemed to have tunnel vision on the Ramseys. However, Mr. Smit would engage in questionable actions himself. He spoke with the Ramseys outside of the official investigation and even prayed with them at one point. During John Ramsey's June 1998 interview, Mr. Smit told John Ramsey he thought someone used a stun gun on JonBenét. Mr. Smit also admitted to Detective Steve Thomas he was aware of Patsy Ramsey telling Pam Griffin she wrote the practice ransom note; yet, he had not written a report regarding this critical piece of information. [During subsequent interviews, the police were unable to confirm that Patsy told Pam Griffin she wrote the practice note. The DA's Office would not force her to testify.] In the end, just as Steve Thomas had done, Mr. Smit submitted a comprehensive resignation letter containing information that undermined the investigation and impaired any future court proceedings.

The Boulder DA's Office turned over considerable case information to the Ramseys and the media. When close friends of the Ramseys, Fleet and Priscilla White, provided sensitive information to District Attorney Alex Hunter, it showed up almost verbatim in the newspaper within a week. John Ramsey stated he called Alex Hunter at home to discuss matters pertaining to the case. Alex Hunter regularly met with and discussed the Ramsey case with a tabloid reporter (Jeff Shapiro, *Globe*), which showed a complete lack of professionalism and ethics! The legality of some of the DA's actions was questionable at best. Lawrence Schiller, author of *Perfect Town Perfect Murder*, claimed his source in the DA's Office gave him over 1,500 pages of official documents (Schiller 1999). The DA's Office was unable to keep confidential information, confidential.

The actions by some of the attorneys within the Boulder DA's Office materially impacted the ability to ever take this case to court. There was a pervasive lack of professionalism throughout the investigation by the Boulder County attorneys. The combination of behaviors by the police and prosecuting attorneys resulted in utter hatred between the two groups, which provided a huge advantage to the Ramseys regarding their freedom, but not pertaining to seeking justice for JonBenét.

Federal Bureau of Investigation ("FBI")

In the early hours of December 26, 1996, the police believed JonBenét had been kidnapped. As a result, the Boulder Police Department called the FBI to assist. Once the "kidnapping" became a murder, the FBI shifted to an advisory role. The FBI provided counsel and suggestions on how to approach the case. Though many in the FBI believed the crime exuded familiarity; thus, someone close to JonBenét perpetrated the murder/cover-up, they maintained their objectivity and professionalism throughout the investigation.

The Ramseys & Legal Team

The Ramsey's initial reactions and behaviors after the brutal murder of their daughter have to be evaluated in the context of the stress they endured. Regardless of their involvement or lack of involvement, they were grieving parents. However, as time passed, their behavior transitioned from reactionary to calculation. Many of their statements and decisions cast blame on friends and acquaintances without any basis. Though appalled when accusations were directed at them the Ramseys causally blamed many people for the heinous acts surrounding the death of JonBenét. They tried to use the media to manipulate the investigation and public opinion. Some of the behaviors and responses were understandable while others were deplorable.

The Ramsey legal team was composed of lawyers, investigators, public relations personnel, and other consultants and experts. The lawyers' sole mission was to keep the Ramseys out of prison. They achieved their objective, but at a huge cost to the Ramseys. The lawyers bullied the police and DA's Office. The Ramsey lawyers set conditions for interviews and ensured any interactions with the Ramseys and police were advantageous to their clients. As a result, the Ramseys always had a slight edge by having critical information before interviews and maintaining some level of control within the interviewing process. Notwithstanding, the lawyers' tactics resulted in the Ramseys appearing guilty to the police and general public throughout most of the publicized portion of the investigation. The Ramsey's evasion of the police drove them near bankruptcy and placed tremendous emotional distress upon them. In the end, it is for the Ramseys to determine whether their approach was worth the cost.

The Ramseys hired private investigators within days of JonBenét's death. The Ramseys later argued that investigators were utilized to find the killer(s) because of the Boulder Police Department's incompetence. However, some accounts indicate investigators hired by the Ramseys interviewed Fleet and Priscilla White on December 27, 1996, just one day after their daughter's death. This occurred well before the evidence of clear tension between the Ramseys and the police surfaced or incompetence was obvious. Therefore, the investigators initially were investigating for reasons other than finding the killer. The investigators also focused on keeping the Ramseys out of prison. The investigators significantly interfered with the official investigation by confusing witnesses and possibly generating conflicting answers from them.

The Ramsey team identified leads pointing toward an intruder. There were easily explainable and justifiable reasons why the Ramseys would want their investigators and attorneys to assist police with the investigation. However, many of the leads presented by the Ramsey team appeared disingenuous and misleading. Many of the suggested avenues of investigation were obviously incorrect and could have easily been resolved by one or both of the Ramseys. For example, the Ramsey team claimed the garrote (part of the instrument used to strangle JonBenét) came from outside the Ramsey house. Later, they backed away from this claim once the police determined the garrote came from inside the house (Wecht 1998). It was not clear what the Ramseys really believed about the origin of the garrote, but most of their stances shielded them from blame rather than provided an accurate depiction of the circumstances.

Police identified the garrote as a component of Patsy's painting supplies. The garrote was a broken piece of a paint brush. The remainder of the paint brush handle was found in a tray right outside the basement wine cellar. According to the house-keeper, Linda Hoffman-Pugh, she placed the painting supplies on the floor outside the wine cellar two days prior to the murder while cleaning the house. The police were unable to account for some fragments of the handle, but there is no information on exactly how much of the handle is missing.

Ramsey lawyers also claimed the pry marks next to a door at the Ramsey house demonstrated the involvement of an intruder. Later, a witness came forward who told police she noticed and told Patsy Ramsey about the pry marks months before the murder. Apparently, the communications within the Ramsey team were as deficient as their communications with the police.

The Ramseys hired many other consultants and experts to counter police claims and prepare for a trial. The Ramsey experts may have indirectly been trying to find the killer through attempts to prove the innocence of the Ramsey family, but they were there to protect their clients. They were part of a massive, expensive team designed to obfuscate the official investigation and sway public opinion. They succeeded on one count and failed miserably on the other. The actions of the Ramsey team may have been legal, but they breached many ethical standards during their plight.

Media

The mainstream and tabloid media exerted themselves as more than a mere reporter of facts. The media became part of the story, which unfortunately, is not uncommon. The media has a long history of gravitating toward influencing public opinion rather than maintaining objectivity. Furthermore, once a media outlet has placed a spin or slant on a story it rarely changes, regardless of the facts.

The media wanted to convict John and Patsy Ramsey from the beginning. There were significant reasons for the media to cast suspicion toward the Ramseys. The media saw the murder of JonBenét as a conduit for generating significant increases in viewership and readership. The media, especially the tabloids, violated many ethical realms and some legal boundaries with their tactics for gathering information. Sadly, the media's behavior was not uncommon or extraordinary; they just raised it to a new level with the widespread interest in the Ramsey case.

The reporting on the Ramsey case slanted strongly toward the guilt of John and Patsy Ramsey. The effect on their lives was without a doubt, catastrophic. Though the Ramseys witnessed their reputations and dignity washed away by the media, John and Patsy actively engaged the media from the very beginning. In the Ramsey's book, *The Death of Innocence*, they described how they were fearful of the media, yet at the same time they continued to seek out the media for interviews and comments (Ramsey 2001). The media failed to honor any kind of professional ethics throughout the coverage of JonBenét's murder investigation, though this was of little surprise to anyone but the Ramseys.

John and Patsy Ramsey's reaction to JonBenét's murder increased public interest. Most of their reactions and behaviors were illogical. The parents refused to cooperate with the police. After telling the police they were too distraught to be interviewed, John and Patsy chose to do an interview on *CNN*.

Witnesses and even potential suspects cooperated with the police. One of their primary reasons for the Ramsey's lack of cooperation was they believed they were suspects; however, there were many people who agreed to police interviews even though the police considered them potential suspects. The police initially viewed everyone around JonBenét suspiciously. Detectives assessed business associates of John Ramsey, neighbors, friends, and people who had worked at the house as possible perpetrators of the murder. Sadly, many of these people were suspected because the Ramseys identified them as suspects to the police. And most of these individuals realized they were being evaluated as possible suspects after multiple interviews, and being asked to provide hand-writing, hair, and blood samples. It did not deter them from cooperating with the police. Unlike the Ramseys, they understood an investigative process needed to unfold. Even though the Ramseys retained lawyers, they could have still cooperated.

Within days of the murder, Fleet White, a friend of the Ramseys, was in John Ramsey's face yelling his moral objections to how the Ramseys were handling the investigation. Fleet demonstrated complete outrage toward John because of his failure to assist the authorities. Fleet was also extremely concerned by the fact that John had hired attorneys, investigators, and public relations personnel, but failed to complete the most basic interviews with the police. The Ramsey's reacted by directing the police toward Fleet and Priscilla White as potential suspects.

Friends and neighbors of the Ramseys were not surprised that they would need to be eliminated as potential suspects. They realized their proximity to JonBenét and other circumstances would lead a reasonable person to believe they would need to be cleared. The Ramseys were completely incapable of understanding this. The Ramseys only wanted to deal with "objective" investigators. The Ramsey's defined someone as an objective investigator if he/she believed they were not involved in their daughter's death. In the Ramsey's book, *The Death of Innocence*, they described investigators who believed the Ramseys perpetrated their daughter's murder as inexperienced while they described anyone who believed they were innocent as highly capable and seasoned (Ramsey 2001).

The Ramseys had many motivations keeping them from demonstrating objectivity. Their primary objective was to stay out of prison. They also desired to save face with the public. None of the Ramsey's actions decreased the suspicion surrounding them. Not surprisingly, avoiding the police, and holding television interviews did not lead to the police removing them from suspicion. Throughout the entire investigation, John and Patsy exhibited all of the characteristics of guilty persons. It does not mean they are guilty, but it is hard for someone to ignore their behavior. It must be evaluated and understood; it cannot be overlooked.

Chapter 3 – The 911 Call

After John Ramsey's initial reading of the ransom note, he instructed Patsy Ramsey to call the police. At 5:52 a.m. on December 26, 1996, Patsy dialed 9-1-1. She called from the kitchen phone on the main floor of the house. While Patsy made the call, John was in his underwear on the floor in the hallway next to the kitchen. He carefully read the ransom note.

In a hysterical state, Patsy had the following conversation with the operator:

> Patsy Ramsey: Police.
>
> 911: What's going on ma'am?
>
> Patsy Ramsey: 755 15th Street.
>
> 911: What's going on there ma'am?
>
> Patsy Ramsey: We have a kidnapping. Hurry, please!
>
> 911: Explain to me what's going on. Ok?
>
> Patsy Ramsey: There. We have a, there's a note left and our daughter's gone.

911: A note was left and your daughter's gone?

Patsy Ramsey: Yes!

911: How old is your daughter?

Patsy Ramsey: She's 6 years old. She's blonde, 6 years old.

911: How long ago was this?

Patsy Ramsey: I don't know I just got the note, and my daughter's gone.

911: Does it say who took her?

Patsy Ramsey: What?

911: Does it say who took her?

Patsy Ramsey: No! I don't know. There's a, there's a ransom note here.

911: It's a ransom note?

Patsy Ramsey: It says 'SBTC. Victory! Please!'

911: Okay, what's your name? Are you Kath...?

Patsy Ramsey: Patsy Ramsey, I'm the mother. Oh my God! Please!

911: Okay, I'm sending an officer over OK?

Patsy Ramsey: Please!

911: Do you know how long she's been gone?

Patsy Ramsey: No I don't! Please we just got up and she's not here. Oh my god! Please!

911: Okay, Cal....

Patsy Ramsey: Please send somebody.

911: I am honey.

Patsy Ramsey: Please.

911: Take a deep breath and...

Patsy Ramsey: Hurry, hurry, hurry!

911: Patsy? Patsy? Patsy? Patsy?

Patsy stated she did not rehearse prior to making the 911 call. Though, it would not have been inappropriate for her to think about what she wanted to say. As Patsy stated in her official interview in June of 1998, "It's not the time to sit down and write out a script." During the call, certain information would need to be conveyed, and if not, the response may be delayed or the wrong people may respond. Patsy stated, she did not think, she just reacted. Though Patsy stated she did nothing to prepare for this call, at the very least she thought about what she was going to say prior to picking up the phone.

During the 911 call, Patsy stated, "our daughter's gone" and later in the call she said, "my daughter's gone." Patsy chose to say that her daughter was "gone" versus "not there." Gone means departed or left. It also means passed away or dead (McClish 2001). Most people would say "not here" because they do not know if she is gone, they only know she is not here. Since neither John nor Patsy even looked for JonBenét, "not here" would have been more appropriate. Patsy may have subconsciously provided more insight into what she knew at that time.

Patsy's knowledge of the ransom note varied considerably depending on the situation. Most of the time, her responses indicated she had barely read the note and had no idea of its contents. Occasionally, her responses indicated she had a greater knowledge of the ransom note.

During the call, the 911 operator asked Patsy who took her daughter. This question caught Patsy off guard. In contrast to her hysterical demeanor prior to this question, Patsy calmly responded, "What?" The operator then repeated the question. Not sure what to do with the question, Patsy let the operator know there was a ransom note. Patsy followed with the statement, "It says SBTC. Victory! Please!"

Patsy gave the operator the sign-off of the ransom note, "…SBTC Victory!" Under the tremendous stress of the situation, Patsy got the acronym correct. This is not an easy acronym to remember. Under stress-free circumstances, I read the note several times and was unable to accurately recite the ending acronym. I also asked numerous people to do the same thing. None of them could recite the acronym correctly. I have also told various persons the note sign-off, and then I immediately asked them to repeat it to me. No one could recite the correct letters in the correct order. For one thing, the acronym is hard to say, almost like a tongue twister. Notwithstanding, Patsy got the acronym exactly right.

Patsy stated she scanned the note on the morning of the 26th, and she looked at the end of the note to see who wrote it. This is one explanation for her reciting the acronym sign-off correctly, though it would require her memory to have been impeccable at a time when she was hysterical and, in her own words, "out of her mind!" Numerous other statements indicated she had very little recollection of the day's events.

Patsy could have been looking over John's shoulder while he read the note. It is not exactly clear when John was on the floor reading the note, or how close he was to Patsy, but it is possible she looked at the note while on the phone. Lighting would have been a factor, but the lighting was sufficient for John to read the note. However, if she read the note as she spoke to the 911 operator then she would not have gotten the sign-off backwards. The note stated, "Victory! S.B.T.C," as opposed to the opposite order Patsy conveyed to the 911 operator, "S.B.T.C Victory!" In her response to the question of who wrote the note, Patsy's tone was less stressed and her reaction had less emotion than her other responses. She had to concentrate, which caused her to let go of her "hysteria." It also lowered her protective guard. She responded without fully processing, thus providing critical insight into her knowledge of the ransom note. Patsy was more familiar with the note than she overtly indicated.

During the 911 call, Patsy also referred to the note as a ransom note. The request for money is located in the second paragraph of the ransom note, past where Patsy had indicated she read that morning. The unscripted nature of the 911 call resulted in Patsy providing way more information than she intended. Her answers demonstrated a good knowledge of the ransom note contents, well beyond what she should have known from a mere scanning of the document.

When Patsy hung up the phone, the receiver did not end the call. Various federal law enforcement agencies, to include the Federal Bureau of Investigation and United States Secret Service completed an analysis on the call. Neither organization's analysis detected any additional voices or noise at the end of the call. At the request of the Boulder Police Department, Aerospace Corporation performed a comprehensive analysis, which identified additional conversation after the end of the "official" 911 call.

Since several federal law enforcement agencies were unable to detect the additional conversation, many question the analysis and subsequent conclusion. Aerospace Corporation claimed to have more advanced technology than the federal agencies that analyzed the 911 tape, which accounted for its ability to detect voices others could not.

According to various sources, Aerospace Corporation detected three distinct voices. Further analysis determined the following statements were uttered at the end of the 911 tape:

John Ramsey: We're not speaking to you!

Patsy Ramsey: Help me Jesus, help me Jesus.

Burke Ramsey: Well, what did you find?

Though the analysis is debatable, there are serious implications if it is accurate. Both John and Patsy stated no one else was present during or after the 9-1-1 call. The captured statements would indicate the Ramseys lied about who was present during and after the 911 call. A remote possibility is both of them somehow blocked this out or could not recall Burke's presence, due to the stress and anxiety of the situation. If the latter is the case, all of John and Patsy's recollections from the morning of December 26, 1996 would be called into question. This is an unlikely scenario. If only one of them were present, then it would be possible he or she could have forgotten, but it is unlikely both of them would have synchronized memory loss.

Assuming Burke was present at the end of the 911 call, John and Patsy may have deceived the authorities in order to keep Burke out of the investigation for his emotional well-being. The parents decided it would not be detrimental to the case to speak for Burke and keep his input to a minimum. Right or wrong, John and Patsy may have believed Burke did not hear anything; therefore, his statements or involvement would not move the investigation forward. Ultimately, if the analysis is accurate, the parental decision kept the investigators away from Burke, thus achieving their desired outcome.

Chapter 4 – 755 15ᵗʰ Street

The former Ramsey house is located at 755 15th Street in Boulder, Colorado in a quaint neighborhood as one drives up a hill toward the mountains to the west. It sits on a small quarter acre lot bunched in between two houses and an alley. It was built in 1927, but it has undergone many renovations and additions, which have significantly reduced the size of the yard, and the house comes close to touching the neighbor's house to the north. The numerous additions generated close to 7,000 square feet of livable space over three stories and a basement. The house has five bedrooms and eight bathrooms.

Many Boulder home tours featured the Ramsey house, which afforded numerous strangers access to the house. The Ramseys had parties on December 15th and December 23rd, 1996 with approximately 150 and 30 guests attending, respectively. The home tours provided an opportunity for strangers to preview the complex floor plan, but the combination of home tours and parties also meant that hundreds of persons entered the Ramsey house in the weeks and months leading up to the death of JonBenét, thus greatly increasing the possibility evidence unrelated to the murder became part of the investigation.

The mistakes made by law enforcement on December 26th alone could fill a book. Those mistakes resulted in extensive contamination of the crime scene. For example, during the morning of December 26th, the police allowed victim advocates and family friends to clean counters in the kitchen, eliminating critical evidence. The law enforcement errors were further compounded by the lack of judgment and discretion shown by the Boulder District Attorney's Office as chronicled exhaustively in Steve Thomas' book, *JonBenét – Inside the Ramsey Murder Investigation.*

JonBenét was the first murder of 1996 in Boulder, Colorado. Over the previous several years the police had been inundated with a culture of softer, kinder policing. The DA's Office had a laissez faire approach to criminal prosecution. In understanding what happened prior to discovery of JonBenét's body, one must be cognizant of the contamination element, the failure to follow basic police procedures, and the overall Boulder culture toward law enforcement and crime in general.

Though most crime scenes are handled more carefully than the Ramsey house, only about 60 – 65% of murders are ever solved. A lack of evidence, conflicting evidence, and/or an inability to establish motive can result in many murders going unsolved. High-profile cases receive greater scrutiny. As a result, errors are amplified. The Ramsey investigation suffered from all of the above listed trademark problems of unsolved murders.

Countless police, paramedics, and other official individuals entered the crime scene on December 26, 1996. As the day progressed, the number of people entering and exiting 755 15th Street grew exponentially. The contamination by this much foot traffic immeasurably impaired the integrity of the crime scene. It is not clear what items law enforcement and family friends moved versus items moved in conjunction with the murder and cover-up.

A neighbor of the Ramseys heard a scream between midnight and 2:00 a.m. on the night of December 25[th,] though the Ramseys did not hear anything during the night. There are many plausible explanations for this. The acoustics within the house may have prevented sound from carrying up the stairwells while allowing it to flow outside of the house. However, on the morning of December 26th, John could hear Patsy screaming from two floors down, but they did not hear JonBenét being *forcefully* removed from her room the previous night. When Patsy screamed for John, he was in the bathroom, and Patsy was most likely in the stairwell, which may have improved the flow of sound through the house.

Acoustic tests conducted in the house showed it was possible to hear sound generated inside the house more clearly from outside than inside the house. No definitive conclusions can be drawn from a neighbor hearing a scream, which may or may not have come from the Ramsey house. To further complicate matters, the neighbor first denied hearing anything during the night. Later she claimed she lied because she did not want to get involved. No one has doubted the neighbor's motives one way or the other, but not wanting to help in the murder of an innocent child is hard to fathom. The absence of common sense and morals was almost a requirement for involvement in the Ramsey case.

During the official interviews with John and Patsy Ramsey, one of the exercises they performed involved identifying unusual items within various pictures taken in and around their house. This exercise was designed to help law enforcement understand what may have been involved in the murder or incidental to the murder. The identification process takes on a different meaning when the police ask a potential suspect versus a witness or victim. An investigator tends to believe the statements of a witness or victim. The initial presumption is an interviewee is presenting a truthful explanation. When a potential suspect is asked to identify photos from the crime scene, the answers may be an attempt to deceive. Moreover, a potential suspect may use his answers to divert the authorities away from the means or motives behind the attack.

One of the items shown in the pictures, and identified as unusual, was an aluminum baseball bat. Police found the bat outside the "butler's door" on the side of the Ramsey house. John Fernie found the butler's door unlocked when he arrived at the Ramsey house on the morning of December 26th. The butler's door is in close proximity to where the ransom note was found, and it would be a logical (a term used loosely within the circumstances of this crime and subsequent investigation) exit point for an intruder. A baseball bat found outside would lead investigators to believe someone left the house.

Three factors may indicate the baseball bat was involved in the murder of JonBenét. First, fibers from carpeting in the basement were found on the baseball bat. Second, during the night of the 25th a neighbor reported hearing a sound described as metal scraping, which could have been the aluminum bat hitting against the house or patio. Third, the bat was found near a likely exit point for an intruder. Under the theory of a cover-up, the placement of the baseball bat would serve as a convenient location to facilitate the perception someone left the house.

No one has definitively determined how or what inflicted the trauma to JonBenét's skull. Theories have included the use of a: flashlight, golf club, baseball bat, etc. Others have speculated the injury was a result of JonBenét falling or being pushed against the sharp edge of a hard, stable object, such as a bathroom counter. No one theory has surpassed the others in this arena. Based on the shape of the head trauma, the flashlight most closely matches the shape of the injury. A golf club or sharp edge would most probably have punctured the skin; therefore, the likelihood either of them caused the blunt trauma is low.

If a cover-up transpired, the baseball bat may have been part of the staging. The baseball bat may or may not have been utilized to strike JonBenét's head, but the bat's location and fibers tying it to the basement, may indicate someone wanted it to look like it was part of the murder. The placement of the baseball bat would illustrate a perpetrator leaving the house. If an intruder placed the ransom note on the back spiral staircase, the butler door would have been one of the most likely options for leaving the house.

If someone used the baseball bat to strike JonBenét, it would be illogical for an intruder to carry the bat out of the house just to leave it where it could easily be found. However, almost all of the other instruments utilized to carry out the crime were left in close proximity to the body. Therefore, the baseball bat was at least removed from the immediate crime scene.

During her June 1998 interviews, interviewers asked Patsy about the baseball bat located outside of the butler's door. She responded it was "...very strange and unusual." She referred to the location of the baseball bat as *unusual* four times. Children leave toys and sporting goods everywhere, yet Patsy was alarmed by the placement of the baseball bat. It might not have been a normal play area, but it would be a reasonable place for a child to leave a toy or sporting good item. If Patsy would have stated the bat's location was *not normal*, it would have been a more expected answer. The placement of a baseball bat outside the house would be an easy way to perpetuate the story of an intruder leaving. The baseball bat would be easy to stage; it would not require anyone to actually leave the house, but it would still provide the appearance an intruder left the house.

Patsy demonstrated no concern regarding the flash light photographed on the kitchen counter. She stated its placement in the kitchen was odd, but at the same time she explained it away by indicating John may have used it to look in the garage. Patsy indicated it looked like a flashlight John Andrew [John's son from a previous marriage] gave to John. It is also possible one of the dozens of police officers who were at the Ramsey house left the flashlight.

The investigators could not account for many components of the crime scene. Any unaccounted for item has been utilized by intruder theorists as validation of one or more intruders, except for the baseball bat, which seems to have escaped them. Though it could be argued some of the fibers, footprints, or moved items were the result of an unknown intruder(s), it is not likely all of them were. One such example is the "unexplained" palm print on the cellar door. There were three palm prints found on the cellar door and two of them were found to be Patsy's. The third print was the one in question. For years, investigators were unable to locate the person who matched this print. However, recent accounts indicate the print tied to Melinda Ramsey [John's daughter from a previous marriage]. Fortunately, this lead was eventually resolved, but the lack of crime scene preservation generates many unanswered questions.

Chapter 5 – The Autopsy Report

Dr. John Meyer, Office of the Boulder County Coroner, conducted the autopsy and corresponding report on JonBenét Ramsey on December 27, 1996. Dr. Meyer performed a cursory external review of the body on December 26, 1996. Initially, the coroner's office only released partial segments of the report. The report described the cause of death as "asphyxia by strangulation associated with craniocerebral trauma."

The fracture on the side of JonBenét's head was around 8.5 inches in length with a rectangular-shaped "displaced fragment" near the end of the fracture. Based primarily on the analysis conducted by Dr. Cyril Wecht, the blow to the side of JonBenét's head occurred either near death or shortly thereafter. This is based on the finding of minimal blood (seven to eight cc's) in the capillaries, which is approximately the amount of residual blood expected in the area at death. As a result, JonBenét was most probably strangled prior to the strike to the head. The person who delivered the blow to her head may or may not have known if JonBenét was still alive or not (Wecht 1998).

The autopsy report identified brain swelling. Dr. Wecht asserted that if JonBenét was alive when she was struck by the blunt object it would have killed her almost instantly. She would have died before the swelling occurred. As a result, the brain swelling came from the strangulation. The strangulation took place first, which allowed for the swelling of JonBenét's brain as she slowly passed away.

There was no skin underneath JonBenét's fingernails, which would most likely indicate she did not struggle. Strangulation victims usually bite their tongues, but there were no injuries to her tongue or checks. JonBenét did not resist. Based on these conditions, JonBenét was likely unconscious at the time she was strangled.

There was minimal to no damage to the interior portion of her neck. The limited damage to the neck could imply an unintentional strangulation. Dr. Wecht asserted there was bruising to the temporal lobe without corresponding external injuries. Therefore, he postulated this may have been the result of shaking JonBenét, which could have been an attempt to wake the child after she passed out (Wecht 1998). Her death was likely accidental.

According to the autopsy report, JonBenét was sexually molested near the time of death. As stated before, JonBenét was strangled, but she did not resist. A postulated theory asserted an intruder removed JonBenét from her room through the use of a stun gun. This could explain her unconsciousness at the time she was strangled. Though, the strangulation could have been part of the sexual molestation, which could have unintentionally caused her to pass out. JonBenét may have believed the rope would not severely hurt her so she did not initially resist. She thought it was part of a game. This does not imply in any way she was okay with what happened to her, but she may have felt it was just something she would have to endure. As the rope tightened around her neck, JonBenét could have easily passed out before she realized her loss of consciousness was imminent.

The person strangling her as part of his sexual gratification may not have realized the tightness of the rope around JonBenét's neck. If one has ever engaged in Jiu-Jjitsu or a similar grappling sport where choking is allowed, one does not always realize when he is about to pass out. Sometimes the lack of blood flow to the brain alerts one to the imminent loss of consciousness, but other times it occurs before one is aware of the likelihood.

Therefore, JonBenét may not have known she was about to lose consciousness. She may not have fully understood the danger she was encountering.

Only after it was too late did the perpetrator realize he seriously hurt or killed JonBenét. He then shook JonBenét, attempting to wake her. Thus, the aggressive sexual act turned into a deadly game. At that time, the individual either panicked or in a rage, struck her with a blunt instrument causing significant trauma to the side of her head. There is no solid information pointing toward any one weapon or object.

In the autopsy report, Dr. Meyer identified the presence of chronic inflammation of the vagina wall. According to Dr. Cyril Wecht, chronic inflammation would most likely indicate an injury was several days old, as an older injury would have healed (Wecht 1998). Therefore, the information indicated JonBenét had trauma to her vagina prior to the night of her death. Also, the hymen was almost non-existent, which could also indicate prior trauma.

The sexual abuse of JonBenét prior to the night of her death could be completely unrelated to her demise. The person(s) who previously molested her may not have been the person who took her life. The circle of suspects for a prior molestation is considerably smaller than the universe of suspects who have been evaluated regarding her death. According to John and Patsy Ramsey, no one had an opportunity to molest JonBenét. There are several ways to evaluate this response. The parents, understandably, could have been in denial. The parents may not have been able to comprehend the statement in light of the already tragic events surrounding their child's death. Another option is one or both of the parents had prior knowledge of the sexual abuse and wish to avoid discussing it. *As a note, there has been no information obtained during the investigation indicating any prior sexual abuse or inappropriate acts by anyone in the immediate Ramsey family.* Nevertheless, prior sexual abuse is a possible explanation for why the parents would not cooperate with the police and obfuscate the investigation.

In the three years leading up to JonBenét's death, she saw her pediatrician a staggering 27 times. Of the visits, 24 related to colds and other more routine childhood ailments. The other three visits involved the complaint of pain while urinating. Her doctor felt the vaginal inflammation resulted from either bubble bath irritation or poor hygiene (Wecht 1998). A young child getting a urinary tract infection or similar problem is not uncommon. Also, many children who have a urinary tract infection may be more prone to them. This could be explained as a potential problem with the kidneys or some other medical condition. It could have also been a result of sexual contact, which would have been highly inappropriate at six years of age or younger.

It has been argued that if JonBenét were to have been taken to the emergency room rather than a doctor's office for the above listed symptoms, the emergency room doctor would have been required to notify the authorities regarding possible child molestation due to the circumstances. Though many of the symptoms could be explained innocently, an appearance of impropriety existed. Under different circumstances, possibly if this happened anywhere other than Boulder, there would have been further inquiries into JonBenét's symptoms.

Upon learning of likely prior vaginal penetration, JonBenét's pediatrician stated he never saw any evidence of her being molested. He indicated if he would have found any evidence indicating wrong-doing, he would have reported it immediately to the proper authorities. Of course, if her doctor acknowledged he suspected something was wrong with JonBenét and he failed to alert the authorities, he would have significant culpability. Her pediatrician has a vested interest in confirming he never suspected any wrong-doing against JonBenét.

JonBenét's doctor was a family friend of the Ramseys (Thomas 2000). Seeing JonBenét's problems could be explained through common events, coupled with the doctor's relationship with the family would make it less likely he would suspect something inappropriate. This is not a judgment on the doctor's professionalism or skill level, but merely a likely possibility when taking into account human nature.

JonBenét's doctor must stay with his original diagnosis as he would be more liable, otherwise. At this point, JonBenét's doctor is no longer objective. He may wish he made further inquiries, but now he must affirm what he has done. He probably followed protocol, but in light of the evidence indicating molestation before the night of JonBenét's death, additional inquiries by her doctor may have uncovered inappropriate activity beforehand. Based on the autopsy, it is not clear how long the molestation had been going on, as it may have only occurred over several days before her death; therefore, it would not have been anything JonBenét's doctor could have uncovered.

Through the child beauty pageants and her associated outfits, JonBenét was sexualized, even if she did not know it. She had bedwetting issues. She went to the doctor on three occasions for urinary-related issues. None of these factors definitively indicate she was molested prior to the night of December 25, 1996. However, the autopsy report indicated she was likely violated prior to the night in question. The evidence of prior molestation is not conclusive, as other things could have caused it, but it is likely. There is no indication previous sexual molestation had anything to do with her death. Though, if her death was a result of a sexual game going too far, it raises the likelihood there may be a connection between previous molestation and what occurred on the night of JonBenét's death.

Fibers were found in the outer portion of JonBenét's vagina, which has prompted many to believe someone wiped the area subsequent to her murder as part of the cover-up. There is no indication anyone has identified the object utilized to wipe her after the attack. There is no specific mention of fibers removed from this area in the autopsy report. The fibers could have also been the result of someone rubbing against her during the molestation. It remains another perplexing element of the crime.

The autopsy report pointed rather strongly toward previous sexual abuse of JonBenét. Though evidence should be challenged, ignoring evidence not matching a specific theory will lead to only believing evidence validating one's existing theory. The likelihood of prior sexual abuse cannot be ignored in this case.

The autopsy provided information on how JonBenét died, but it did not provide enough detail to point definitively toward any one person or even one act. The most critical information gathered from the autopsy report was the minimal blood found in the capillaries around the head wound, indicating the blow to the side of her head occurred after or near death. It almost eliminated the possibility the strangulation component was part of the cover-up; it most likely caused her death. As a result, the accident shifts from a potential fall to a sexual scenario that went too far.

The autopsy report stated the, "Small intestines contains fragmented pieces of yellow to light green-tan...which may represent fragments of pineapple." This statement has presented one of the most perplexing pieces of evidence in the case. Investigators and intruder theorists alike

acknowledge pineapple was found in JonBenét's
intestines. It should be noted the autopsy reports
stated the items found *may* represent pineapple.
Though later testing indicated the contents were
conclusively pineapple. The presence of pineapple
presented a significant obstacle to the pure intruder
theory, limiting the perpetrator(s) to persons
JonBenét knew well.

Chapter 6 – Pineapple

To add to the already confusing and murky circumstances surrounding the death of JonBenét, the coroner found pineapple in JonBenét's small intestines during the autopsy. According to various interviews, no pineapple was served at Fleet and Priscilla White's party on Christmas evening, and no one at the party saw JonBenét eating pineapple. The Ramseys were at the White's from approximately 4:30 p.m. until 8:30 p.m. Both John and Patsy Ramsey stated JonBenét did not have anything to eat upon their arrival home that night. According to various accounts from one of Burke Ramsey's interviews, he indicated JonBenét did not eat after their arrival home that night.

Trying to tie JonBenét's consumption of pineapple into a viable chronology of events has proven rather challenging. The presence of pineapple almost eliminates the possibility of a stranger abducting, molesting, and killing JonBenét. Once strangers have been eliminated, it only leaves persons who knew JonBenét. To conjure up a scenario where an individual fed her pineapple, the individual had to know her very well. As a result, some intruder theorists discredit the presence of pineapple in her intestines. However, reports regarding the testing results state it was definitively pineapple. In their book, the Ramseys describe the presence of pineapple as "an urban legend" (Ramsey 2001). As Agatha Christie wrote in *The Mysterious Affair at Styles*, "Everything must be taken into account. If the fact will not fit the theory---let the theory go." Rather than changing the facts, the theory must be changed. Any legitimate theory regarding the events of December 25, 1996 must account for JonBenét eating pineapple.

The pineapple found in JonBenét's intestines during the autopsy conflicts with most theories about what happened during the night. It does not bolster the intruder theory, as the presumption is JonBenét knew the person well, thus limiting the list of potential intruders. Feeding JonBenét pineapple showed familiarity with her and comfort within the home. For an intruder to sit down at the kitchen table and feed her pineapple in the middle of the night would mean the person was comfortable with JonBenét and would need to have a reason for being there, if caught by the parents. The list of intruders who would potentially fit this type of behavior include: Linda Hoffman-Pugh, Patsy's sisters and parents, and John's children from his previous marriage. All of these individuals have been cleared. Additionally, it would be difficult for any of them to articulate a reason why they would be in the home in the middle of the night without prior notice. There are other individuals who would have been well known to JonBenét, but they would not have been familiar enough with the house to exert this level of comfort.

For an intruder theory involving one or more strangers to be credible, the pineapple must be discredited or explained. Since the testing of the pineapple appears sound, intruder theorists must contend JonBenét had pineapple at the White's house or she ate it on her own upon arriving home that night. It is unlikely, but it is possible a guest could have brought pineapple to the party and was either not interviewed properly or forgot he/she brought pineapple to the White's.

As with all things Ramsey, their answers must be viewed skeptically. It is not clear whether John or Patsy fed JonBenét pineapple. Based on their interview answers in June of 1998, they did not feed her prior to putting her to bed. Needless to say, most likely the Ramseys believed they could not change any portion of their stories without fear of arrest or further accusations of complicity in their daughter's murder. Therefore, even if one of the parents fed JonBenét pineapple they would not be able to admit it.

Patsy indicated JonBenét would not have been able to reach the pineapple bowl herself. She specifically stated Burke would have been able to reach the bowl. Later, Patsy back-tracked from this potential misstatement (Burke comment) by mitigating the likelihood either one of the children would be in the kitchen in the middle of the night. If Patsy accidently slipped in her statement regarding Burke, she quickly took steps to downplay Burke as a possible accomplice to JonBenét during her nighttime pineapple eating escapade.

During Patsy's June 1998 interviews, she mentioned several times the implausibility of Burke and JonBenét being up in the middle of the night. She stated the children getting food in the middle of the night would be highly unusual. She referred to it as "far-fetched." Patsy stated that she would have heard Burke if he was in the kitchen, yet someone was in the kitchen during the night and she claimed to have not heard him or them.

According to various sources, the pineapple in JonBenét's stomach was fresh, not canned. Investigators discovered a bowl of pineapple containing a large wooden spoon in the Ramsey's kitchen on the morning of December 26th. In interviews, both John and Patsy indicated they were not familiar with the spoon, nor would they serve pineapple in the manner depicted in the picture.

The bowl with fresh pineapple in it contained fingerprints from Patsy and Burke. It would have been reasonable to find JonBenét's and/or the house-keeper's fingerprints on the bowl as well, but they were not present. John Ramsey's prints were also absent from the bowl. The five persons listed would all have a legitimate reason to have touched the bowl containing the pineapple. Other friends and family may have had reason to touch the bowl too.

Rest assured if there was an unidentified fingerprint on the bowl of pineapple, intruder theorists would have jumped all over the pineapple angle. Suddenly, the pineapple would become a pivotal piece of evidence. The absence of an unidentified fingerprint does not mean an unidentified person did not touch the bowl, it just means he did not leave a print. The pineapple found its way into JonBenét's digestive system, and understanding how it got there may provide additional insight into the events of December 25th, 1996.

Based on the fingerprints on the bowl, we can follow two pathways surrounding the bowl of pineapple, either others touched the bowl and did not leave prints, or only Burke and Patsy touched the bowl. If one or more individuals touched the bowl, but they did not leave prints then the list of potential individuals is practically limitless. However, due to the likely familiarity necessary in providing a midnight snack, the person or persons had to have been well known to JonBenét.

If the fingerprints tell the story, then either Burke or Patsy prepared and fed JonBenét the pineapple. Patsy almost implicated Burke with her response indicating Burke would have been able to reach the bowl. Prior to thinking of the implication, Patsy probably thought that Burke and JonBenét could have been awake together in the middle of the night. And it would have required her older brother to get the bowl down from the cabinet. Once she realized she opened a scenario she would not be able to fully explain or justify, she changed her statement. She referred to Burke and JonBenét being in the kitchen at night as highly unlikely. It is certainly plausible that either Burke or Patsy could have been awake with JonBenét in the kitchen on the night of December 25th. Did JonBenét go back to bed after eating pineapple or not? Was she removed from her room a second time by another individual, or did the individual who fed her pineapple cause her demise?

Whoever awoke JonBenét that night, likely did so after the family had gone to bed. Based on the location of the pineapple in JonBenét's intestines, she ate the fruit early in the encounter in order for it to move into her intestines prior to her death. According Dr. Cyril Wecht, it would take about two hours for the pineapple to move from the stomach to the small intestines (Wecht 1998). The perpetrator(s) was able to remove JonBenét from her bed and room without force. *This conclusion is derived from the progression of events, which indicate comfort and familiarity, not brute force.* They descended the spiral staircase and headed to the kitchen. They sat in the kitchen while JonBenét ate pineapple.

The perpetrator then took JonBenét to the basement under a ruse or innocent suggestion. She most likely went along willingly as she trusted the individual. Plus, there is no indication of a struggle in the kitchen or anywhere on the first floor. Once they moved into the basement, the comfort and security JonBenét felt toward the individual was quickly washed away as the horrific events started to unfold.

Chapter 7 - Ransom Note

The ransom note is the most critical piece of evidence in the JonBenét Ramsey murder investigation. It is one of the few physical items pulled from the crime scene that we know for certain was part of the crime/cover-up. It provides considerable insight into the thinking of who either killed JonBenét and/or covered-up the crime. There is little within the note and the circumstances around the murder leading one to believe this was a legitimate attempt to kidnap her. The ransom note moves this crime from unthinkable to downright confusing. Initially, it provides more questions than answers.

Around 5:45 a.m. on the morning of December 26, 1996, Patsy Ramsey walked down the back spiral staircase of her home. According to her statements, three pieces of paper were lain out on one of the lower stair rungs. As she stepped over the papers, she turned and started to read them. Immediately upon reading the note, Patsy determined JonBenét had been kidnapped.

Numerous questions surround the note, referred to as, "the *War & Peace* of ransom notes." Why was it written? When was it written? What do all of the ramblings mean? Did the killer write it, or did a different person write the ransom note? All of the evidence surrounding the murder and subsequent cover-up are valuable, but the ransom note provides the context for everything else.

In general, a ransom note conveys what one wants and the conditions around receiving it. An indirect, though equally important aspect of a ransom note requires that it not identity the kidnapper(s). A ransom note usually provides direct, curt instructions to the person responsible for gathering the money, and no information about who is committing the crime. The communications between the kidnappers and the person responsible for obtaining the money are of paramount importance and require extensive planning. Tremendous preparation should go into the communications in order to ensure the orders were followed, money is received, and no one gets caught.

In one of the most famous kidnappings, the abduction of Charles Lindbergh's baby, the child died during the actual kidnapping. The child was still taken with the kidnapper(s), buried, and the ransom was obtained. In contrast, JonBenét died during the supposed kidnapping attempt, but she was left in the house. Many elements surrounding the death of JonBenét differ from what would be expected.

Though the actual kidnappings differed considerably, the Ramsey ransom note had some similarities to the ransom note left at the Lindbergh house. The person who wrote the amateurish note found at the Ramsey house may have been familiar with the first ransom note in the Lindbergh case. The Lindbergh note was written by a man of foreign origins where English was not his first language. The Ramsey note made an initial attempt to attribute the crime to a foreign group and misspelled two words in the early part of the note. The Lindbergh note had extensive misspellings and grammatical errors.

Both notes asked for a specific breakdown of the ransom money among various bills. The Lindbergh and Ramsey notes identified a future time (or date in the case of the Lindbergh note) where arrangements would be made versus a time when an exchange would take place. Further, both notes warned against contacting the police or others. However, the Ramsey note may have used the initial Lindbergh note as a starting point, but the Ramsey ransom note far exceeded the Lindbergh note in length. The Lindbergh note had no additional or superfluous information, whereas the Ramsey note was overly wordy and provided numerous phrases that did not further the objectives of a ransom note.

In a ransom note, one would expect a short note outlying the demands and next steps, accompanied by a person missing. With the JonBenét Ramsey case, we have a dead body and the following:

Mr. Ramsey, Listen carefully! We are a group of individuals that represent a small foreign faction. We ~~xx~~ respect your bussiness but not the country that it serves. At this time we have your daughter in our posession. She is safe and unharmed and if you want her to see 1997, you must follow our instructions to the letter.

You will withdraw $118,000.00 from your account. $100,000 will be in $100 bills and the remaining $18,000 in $20 bills. Make sure that you bring an adequate size attaché to the bank. When you get home you will put the money in a brown paper bag. I will call you between 8 and 10 am tomorrow to instruct you on delivery. The delivery will be exhausting so I advise you to be rested. If we monitor you getting the money early, we might call you early to arrange an earlier delivery of the money and hence, a earlier ~~delivery~~ pickup of your daughter.

Any deviation of my instructions will result in the immediate execution of your daughter. You will also be denied her remains for proper burial. The two gentlemen watching over your daughter do not particularly like you so I advise you not to provoke them. Speaking to anyone about your situation, such as Police, F.B.I., etc., will result in your daughter being beheaded. If we catch you talking to a stray dog, she dies. If you alert bank authorities, she dies. If the money is in any way marked or tampered with, she dies. You will be scanned for electronic devices and if any are found, she dies. You can try to deceive us but be warned that we are familiar with Law enforcement countermeasures and tactics. You stand a 99% chance of killing your daughter if you try to out smart us. Follow our instructions and you stand a 100% chance of getting her back. You and your family are under constant scrutiny as well as the authorities. Don't try to grow a brain John. You are not the only fat cat around so don't think that killing will be difficult. Don't underestimate us John. Use that good southern common sense of yours. It is up to you now John!

Victory!
S.B.T.C

A ransom note, in general, would direct blame for the crime at almost anyone outside of the immediate family, as the immediate family would not be able to extract money from itself, except in the case of an insurance policy payout.

The Ramsey ransom note identified who committed the crime. A "small foreign faction" committed the act. It also had a sign-off of "S.B.T.C." If the ransom note was not designed to deceive then these two items would tell us who attempted to kidnap and subsequently killed JonBenét. A closer look at the ransom note points toward a different suspect group as possible authors. The ransom note was found on a small back stairwell. It was written in the house on a note pad from the kitchen. Consequently, the note perpetuated a cover-up of murder rather than effect a ransom in conjunction with a kidnapping. All of these factors point toward someone very close to JonBenét and most likely someone in the immediate family.

The letter was written to John Ramsey ("Mr. Ramsey"). With the finding of a "practice note," there was a conscious decision to write the note to John Ramsey, since he would likely obtain the ransom money. The formality of "Mr." is odd. By the end of the note "John replaced "Mr." The deception becomes apparent with the inability of the writer to maintain a consistent message throughout the note. Formal to casual. Misspellings to correct spellings. Many of these transitions point toward an inexperienced criminal trying to deceive. As the note progressed, it showed more of the subconscious and true intent of the writer.

At the beginning of the ransom note, the kidnapper showed signs of disorganization; he did not even know to whom to address the letter. One theory states the note was written prior to the murder, as the killer would have been more composed and calm during that time. Nevertheless, the writer confused the intended recipient of the note. The note rambled. It was overly wordy, which seemed to indicate the note was written under duress and not during the hours of downtime an intruder would have had prior to the Ramsey's arriving home from the White's, as has been postulated. Further, if someone other than the killer wrote the note, it mitigates the impact the act of killing would have on the state of the writer. For one to believe an actual kidnapping attempt was made, the note had to have been written prior to the death of JonBenét. If the note was written after the murder then there was never a kidnapping attempt.

The ransom note turned a murder into an apparent botched kidnapping. The note does not change the fact a murder occurred, but it changes the motive. The author had to weigh the benefit of changing the motive against the negatives associated with leaving extensive additional evidence through the writing of a note.

The note was primarily written to direct suspicion away from who actually killed JonBenét. Covering up a murder with a kidnapping would only make sense for someone close to JonBenét, because a kidnapping would imply the work of a stranger or someone outside the immediate family. The ransom note turned whatever actually happened into an act to achieve financial gain.

The ransom note had a secondary motive. It was written to keep John Ramsey from calling the police. The vicious nature of the wording has led many to believe the person hated John. However, only when there is mention of John calling the police or talking to other people does the note take a much more vicious tone. The later portion of the note was designed to keep John from calling the police. There is little information or even conjecture about what would be accomplished by preventing John from calling the police. If John did not call the police, it would buy the perpetrator(s) time. The perpetrator(s) planned to remove the body from the house when John went to the bank to obtain the ransom money. The note specifically stated for John to go to the bank. Therefore, it was critical John did not notify anyone who could prevent the removal of the body from happening.

If the note was written before the murder then it could conceivably have been a legitimate ransom note. If this were the case, one of the most important elements of this plan would be to leave with JonBenét. The perpetrator(s) would have to either contend with removing JonBenét from the residence: 1) while she struggled, 2) convince her to willingly walk out, or 3) incapacitate her by some means. The first option would be quite challenging and probably not the choice selected. Option two would be the most pleasant; however, there would have to be a capability to take her out of the house either by force or by incapacitating her, if necessary. Only under the scenario where the perpetrators came into the house with the sole plan of convincing JonBenét to walk out of the house does the note have any credibility as a means to obtain a ransom. Under this scenario, after JonBenét died the person(s) had no means or ability to take her with him, thus the ransom attempt could only be continued by hiding her body in the house.

Under either of the two other more likely scenarios, JonBenét's body would have been taken with them because they would have had the means to remove her. Without her body, no ransom would be paid. There is no way anyone would believe one could successfully hide a body in the house and be able to extract the ransom money. Granted, it took the Ramseys and the Boulder Police Department over seven hours to find the body, but they eventually found her. Ransom is a highly unlikely or believable motive behind this crime.

There is no reasonable explanation for why an intruder would take JonBenét to the basement. The goal would have been to remove her from the house, even if he wanted to molest her. It would make much more sense for someone within the house to take her to the basement, as it would shield any noise from other occupants of the house.

An intruder(s) would have broken into the house around 5 p.m. or 6 p.m. Otherwise, it is quite improbable an intruder wrote the ransom note sitting at the kitchen table with the entire family in the house. Why did the killer(s) break into a house in order to write the note beforehand? The killer would have been in the house for seven or more hours to complete the crime. There is no reason to be in the house this long. The killer(s) did not enter the house over five hours early in order to understand the floor plan of the house. Clearly, whoever wrote it did not think through the note concept a head of time. It makes no sense for the killer(s) to enter the house so early in the day with the only objectives to be accomplished in five hours were to learn the layout of the house, location of light switches, and write a ransom note. Notwithstanding, if one or more intruders did enter the house, they may have done so hours before the Ramseys returned home for the evening.

One theory postulates the intruders may have left the body behind because they got scared. They quickly climbed out of a basement window to avoid detection. This would counter the calm and drawn out manner of all the other proposed actions during the night. Possibly they heard someone walking around upstairs? Yet, none of the Ramseys got out of bed during the night of December 25; therefore, this is not a likely explanation of events.

If a stranger killed (accidently or not) JonBenét, there is no reason to leave a ransom note. He left the body in the house. Leaving a note would cast suspicion toward a stranger while not leaving a note would cast suspicion on the family. The ransom note does not provide any real value to an intruder other than assisting in a cover- up, which does not benefit an intruder, only an insider.

Upon the discovery of the ransom note, John and Patsy's immediate reactions were particularly interesting. *All of the information gathered regarding the parent's actions/reactions to the ransom note is based on their recollections and willingness to divulge the information.* Patsy, who found the note, immediately screamed for John. When asked why she was so sure JonBenét was gone, Patsy said she had a note saying someone had taken her. At no time did Patsy indicate she questioned the authenticity of the note or its content. According to Patsy, she did not even read the entire note, but merely skimmed it. Patsy almost immediately believed the note.

It was approximately 5:45 a.m. in the morning when Patsy found the note. At that time, she had been awake for about 15 minutes and had not taken a shower or consumed caffeine. She had just awoken. Patsy was clearly not in her most alert state; however, she does not have any disbelief in the note.

Maybe she misread it. Think of all the rationalization spinning through one's mind, trying to come up with a scenario other than what she just read. Maybe it was a joke. Maybe she read it out of order, and it would make more sense if she read it differently. Even though JonBenét had been known to sleep in Burke's room, Patsy was fully convinced someone had taken JonBenét after checking only one room at most. In addition, she did not enter JonBenét's room; she just looked in. JonBenét could have been eating breakfast or sleeping in her playroom. JonBenét could have been in any one of the numerous other rooms Patsy failed to check.

John Ramsey also took the note very seriously. Upon reading the note, he immediately told Patsy to call the police. Though John reacted to the ransom note, he failed to search the house. There was no indication the intruders and/or JonBenét left the house, other than the note. He made no attempt to look for his daughter or to protect his family. At the same time, there was no reason to believe John was privy to what happened during the night. However, he exhibited unusual and counterintuitive behavior.

The Ramseys believed some portions of the note, but not other aspects. The note directed them to not tell anyone or talk to anyone, yet Patsy called several friends. Patsy chose to risk her child's life to have her friends in the house. And Patsy failed to ask anyone she called if they had seen JonBenét. Patsy did not call the Ramsey's friends to assist in finding JonBenét, but to comfort her.

The length of the ransom note is one of its most unique aspects. The writer composed a long, rambling ransom note. There were emotional and stress-related reasons for the length of the note. Maybe the author was long-winded. He provided far more than the basic information. The note was a clear message to John Ramsey. The note told John not to think. It also threatened John numerous times not to call the police.

The note identified the kidnappers as a "group of individuals" that "represent" a "small foreign faction." There was no reason to provide this information. "Represent?" Were the kidnappers acting as attorneys on behalf of this foreign faction? The note's author designed this statement to confuse or deflect the reader away from the true identity of the writer and perpetrator. Moreover, most people would not refer to themselves as "foreign." It is how someone would refer to someone else (McClish 2001).

The phrase "group of individuals" and the word "represent" are words that could be removed from the note and not alter the meaning. Not only does the ransom note seem to address unnecessary topics, it provided excess word usage not necessary to convey the desired point. The note provided excess statements and unnecessary ramblings throughout.

The use of "we" and "two gentlemen" are two other examples where the note tried to confuse the reader regarding the identity of the perpetrator(s) of the crime. Though there may well have been more than one individual (hence, "we") involved in this crime and cover-up, the author chose "we" to convey to the reader the involvement of more than one individual whether it was true or not. The author wanted the reader to believe he wrote the note on behalf of others. This could be done to convey an air of confidence or intimidation, but it was most likely another attempt at distorting the true identity of the person(s) behind the murder.

The overall use of the word "delivery" does not make sense. Kidnappers do not deliver a child to the parents. Normally, kidnappers would tell the parents where to find their child (McClish 2001). This is not the mistake of an inexperienced kidnapper, but of someone who is not intent on completing a kidnapping. The phrasing provided another example of deception.

The ransom note stated "…watching over your daughter." If someone is watching over something or someone they are not keeping a very close eye on the object. "Watching over" implied the two gentlemen are not maintaining a good control over JonBenét. The writer may have known she was already dead, which would explain why someone would not have to ensure she was secured. The ransom note also stated "she dies" four times, which is present tense versus future tense. The wording "she dies" provided further indication the author knew JonBenét was already dead when he wrote the note (McClish 2001).

In the note, the words "business" and "possession" were misspelled. All other words were spelled correctly, including words more difficult to spell. The misspellings took place at the beginning of the note. Most experts believe the words were misspelled on purpose in an attempt to convey an uneducated or unsophisticated writer. The writer also confused "*do* particularly like you." The author had to add the word "not" to the note. This is not a likely mistake to be made by a premeditated kidnapper. More sophisticated words were used later in the note (and spelled correctly), such as "attaché" and "countermeasures." This is additional evidence the note attempted to deceive and obfuscate the true circumstances of the crime.

The note asked for $118,000, which was a fairly small and specific amount. The amount meant something to the note's author. The amount is very close to a bonus (deferred compensation) John Ramsey received earlier in the year. Patsy claimed to be unaware of the amount of the bonus. She further stated she was unaware a bonus was even paid to John earlier in 1996. John also claimed he did not remember the amount of the bonus.

It is not clear whether the ransom amount was put into the note as an attempt to direct the police toward a specific person or persons, or if it was placed in the note at a subconscious level. In either scenario, the likely group of suspect writers would include: select employees at John's work privy to this information, workers in and around the Ramsey household, and the immediate Ramsey family members. The amount could mean nothing, but due to the stress the author would have been under at the time of writing, it was most likely an amount thought to be random, but had some meaning to the author on a subconscious level.

In the second paragraph of the ransom note it stated, "The delivery will be exhausting so I advise you to be rested." This is rather interesting advice coming from a kidnapper. If the note was written during the afternoon/evening of December 25th, the Ramseys were out for the evening, but had a full night's sleep a head of them. The kidnapper(s) would have known the Ramseys would not find the note until the following morning; therefore, the comment was unnecessary. When the note is found, they would already be awake and in the process of finding JonBenét and securing the ransom money. The information makes no sense, unless the "tomorrow" in the note referred to December 27th, then the Ramseys would have had an opportunity to rest.

If the ransom note was written in the middle of the night, the Ramseys were supposedly sleeping. It was completely illogical to advise sleeping people to be rested. Moreover, as with the first scenario, once they found the note they would have no opportunity to rest. The sentence is only made sense if the author of the note referred to himself needing to be rested. And this would point toward a note written in the middle of the night versus in the afternoon.

If the ransom note was written after midnight then "tomorrow" likely referred to the day after the note was found (December 27th). If the note was written while the Ramseys visited the Whites, then tomorrow would have been December 26th. Upon close review, the note's instructions did not make sense if it intended for "tomorrow" to be December 26th.

The note specifically instructed John to go to the bank. The note instructed John to place the money in an attaché then transfer the money to a brown paper bag upon returning home. The note's author then stated he would call between 8:00 a.m. and 10:00 a.m. tomorrow. If tomorrow referred to the 26th then John would have been expected to have found the note, traveled to the bank and returned prior to the 8:00 a.m. to 10:00 a.m. window for the call. The problem is that most banks are not open before 8:00 a.m.; therefore, John most likely would not have had the money by 8:00 a.m. Furthermore, the kidnapper should not have known when the Ramseys would wake up the next day so it is also possible they would not have found the note before 8:00 a.m. The note then went on to state, "If we monitor you getting the money early…" How would John have gotten the money earlier if the note intended for the call to take place on December 26th?

He could not have picked up the money earlier. It only made sense if the time window for the call referred to December 27th. The ransom note further stated if John obtained the money earlier, an earlier pickup would be arranged. However, there was never a set time for picking up JonBenét, so it is not clear to what time/date "earlier" was referring.

It is possible the note's author did intend for "tomorrow" to be December 26th. This would be the case if the note was written on December 25th or even if it was written in the early morning hours of December 26th, as many people associate the time in the middle of the night with the previous day. The next day does not begin until daylight, compared to the actual transition at midnight. Under both scenarios it is clear there was no intent to receive a ransom as none of the instructions made sense if they had to be followed on the 26th. Under no scenario does the note lead one to believe an actual ransom was sought.

The ransom note was written to deceive John Ramsey and later the police. It attempted to deflect blame away from the person(s) who committed the murder. There is no other reason why someone would write a ransom note after killing a little girl who they were not taking with them. It does not change the fact a murder was committed. It only attempted to alter the perception of what happened. The note was written inside the Ramsey house during the commission of a felony. Taking the time to write a ransom note under those conditions placed the individual(s) in a significantly vulncrable position. One could easily have been detected by the Ramseys. A cover-up would be most logical if the death was an accident. There is no indication murder was the objective.

If it were an accident, what would lead to a child dying? Other than a legitimate accident or rage-induced act, the motive may have been sexual in nature. Based on the autopsy and subsequent review by Dr. Cyril Wecht, the blow to the head occurred at or near death, which would lessen the likelihood the head trauma was the accident. Therefore, the strangulation becomes the more likely accidental portion of the incident, which could indicate the perpetrator forced JonBenét into some kind of sexual game involving strangulation. It is plausible, but not likely, someone broke into the house on Christmas night to play sexual games and molest a young girl.

No credibility has been given to the "foreign faction" aspect of the ransom note, including many of the intruder theorists. Yet, many still think the overall note is a legitimate attempt to receive a ransom. The ransom note must have a severability clause. To believe the overall authenticity of the ransom note, one must ignore or discount certain portions of the note while placing greater credibility on other portions. There is no obvious way to definitively identify which portions of the note were genuine. As a result, the overall note lacks credibility as a ransom note. It was a tool of deception.

The ransom note never mentioned "JonBenét's" name. There are two likely reasons for this. Either the writer of the note did not know her name, or it was too painful for the author to write her name. By writing JonBenét's name, the author would be, in essence, acknowledging what happened to her. For someone close to her, the reality of the situation would be too much to bear. Only under a scenario where the writer was a complete stranger would he not know JonBenét's name. Even most intruder theorists believe the person(s) who perpetrated this crime knew the family, if only tangentially. Therefore, it leaves the scenario where the writer intentionally left out JonBenét's name from the note because it caused too much pain to write it, which limits the potential suspects to a small circle around the Ramseys.

There has been minimal debate about where the ransom note was written. It is broadly believed the note was written inside the Ramsey's house. The note was written on a pad of paper from inside the house. The pen also came from inside the house. After the note was written, the note's author placed the pen back in the cup where it was kept. Since someone returned the pen to its appropriate location in the kitchen, the note was most likely written in the kitchen or the immediate surrounding area. It is unlikely someone wrote the note while in the basement and then brought the pen and pad of paper back upstairs to the kitchen area to put it away. It was also quite a polite gesture on the part of the note's author to put the pen back in its appropriate place.

The ransom note conveyed many things. It conveyed familiarity with the family. It conveyed a caring, feminine tone though the harsh threats around what would be done to JonBenét offset that. It also demonstrated an attempt to cover-up what actually happened.

Hand-writing analysis is considered by many as more art than science. Nonetheless, there are strong indications Patsy Ramsey wrote the ransom note. Many hand-writing experts identified Patsy as the writer of the note. The credentials and track record of each expert could be called into question, as could the overall accuracy of hand-writing analysis. Additionally, there is a subjective nature to hand-writing analysis. One suggestion is to blind test the hand-writing samples. This could consist of a team of three or more objective (no prior association with the case or its participants) hand-writing experts to look at all of samples provided to the Boulder Police Department. The experts would not be given any information on the identity of the authors. The experts would analyze the hand-writing samples to see if any of the exemplars match closely to the ransom note. This exercise would go a long way toward validating any conclusions drawn regarding the proposed author of the ransom note. Without having conducted blind testing, the current discussion around the ransom note authorship is focused more on the experts themselves than the conclusions.

Most likely, the note's author attempted to conceal his hand-writing while crafting the note. The author changed the way certain letters were written, spacing, and word choice, which would make it more difficult to match the note to a specific person at a later date. However, a lot of hand-writing is subconscious so many elements of writing will show through regardless of attempts at concealment.

There is much debate about the ability of hand-writing experts to be able to identify an author of a given document. This could also be turned the other way to indicate no one can be excluded by hand-writing experts either. This logic is rather extreme as many people believe they could spot obvious differences in hand-writing without any technical training or experience. Therefore, there is clearly some ability for hand-writing specialists to derive similarities and dissimilarities between writings. Hand-writing analysis can identify patterns and style and even provide an assessment on the identity of the author; however, it most likely provides a confidence level below what would be acceptable to convict someone in a criminal court. Notwithstanding, hand-writing analysis should not be discarded, as it can provide valuable insight.

According to Steve Thomas, detective on the JonBenét Ramsey case, out of the 73 potential suspects whose hand-writing had been evaluated by the time he left the case, all of them had been eliminated as potential writers except Patsy Ramsey. One Colorado Bureau of Investigation ("CBI") examiner stated 24 out of 26 letters in the ransom note matched Patsy's. Several police officers and hand-writing experts believed Patsy altered her hand-writing within the samples provided to the police. When police obtained notes written in the normal course of her life, they varied considerably from what Patsy provided the police in a controlled environment. The significant variations in Patsy's samples made it very difficult to definitively tie her overall writing to the ransom note. This troubling act conveyed the appearance of impropriety.

The most troubling aspect is Patsy Ramsey's left-handed exemplars (right-hand dominant) most closely tied to the ransom note. Patsy never told the authorities she could write left-handed. Only after extensive interviewing did investigators uncover her ambidextrous tendencies. One would have to go to great lengths to innocently explain away how Patsy's left-handed exemplars were the closest match to the writing in the ransom note.

In response to claims her hand-writing could not be excluded as the author of the ransom note, Patsy responded with a very knowledgeable understanding of hand-writing analysis. She claimed her experts, paid by the Ramseys, rated her hand-writing as a 4.5 on a 1 to 5 scale, where 5 is a totally incomplete match. Though it is likely a defense team could find one or more experts who would conclude Patsy's hand-writing does not match the ransom note, most likely some of the experts consulted by the defense team concluded she may have written the note. There were many similarities between Patsy's hand-writing and the ransom note. It is highly unlikely most objective experts could explain away the similarities.

During the *Today Show* in March of 2000, Katie Couric asked Patsy about her authoring the ransom note. Pasty responded:

> When we find the killer, the killer's [handwriting] is going to match much closer than Patsy Ramsey's. There are lots of pieces of handwriting that we have of other suspects that match much more closely than mine does.

The most telling aspect of Patsy's response is she did not deny she wrote the note, nor did she refute that her hand-writing matches the writing in the ransom note. She merely deflected the question by saying the killer will match more closely than her. Patsy also referred to herself in the third person, which can indicate narcissism (inflated self-importance and lack of empathy) in some, though trying to determine Patsy Ramsey's potential for personality disorders would be pure conjecture.

There were many similarities between Patsy's handwriting and the ransom note. Hand-writing experts identified consistencies in Patsy's spelling, grammar, formatting, invention of acronyms, and other traits to those of the ransom note. One detrimental element of Patsy's hand-writing samples is her hand-writing changed after the death of her daughter. Patsy's hand-writing completed before the death of JonBenét compared to hand-writing afterward showed striking contrasts, to include changes in how certain letters were written and the overall style of her writing. For example, Patsy stopped using a manuscript "a" in her writing post-homicide, though she used it all the time prior to JonBenét's murder. *In the ransom note, the manuscript "a" was used 109 times and only five times in the printed format.*

The various hand-writing samples Patsy provided to law enforcement exhibited inconsistencies and changes. Most experts would consider alterations in hand-writing to indicate someone who was trying to disguise her hand-writing. It is unlikely Patsy could have altered her hand-writing unintentionally. More likely, she tried to deceive the hand-writing experts by conveying a writing style different than her normal writing.

In the 1997 Ramsey Christmas letter, Patsy utilized the phrase, "and hence," which was used in the ransom. It was just too close to the ransom note. Patsy claimed she must have picked up the phrase from reading the ransom note so often. Her defenders explained how reading a document several times could translate into the reader's own writings.

At the same time, Pasty claimed she was unfamiliar with the note because it was too painful to read. Around the time of the 1997 Christmas letter, Patsy maintained the stance of almost complete ignorance of the ransom note's content. The defense presented a logical argument, but it was not consistent with Patsy's other statements. The sentence in question bore significant similarities to the same sentence in the ransom note.

> Had there been no birth of Christ, there would be no hope of eternal life, and hence, no hope of ever being with our loved ones again.
> -   1997 Ramsey Christmas letter

> If we monitor you getting the money early, we might call you early to arrange an earlier delivery of the money and hence, a earlier ~~delivery~~ pickup of your daughter.
> -   Ransom note

The Christmas letter sentence was the last sentence of the second paragraph, exactly the same position as the corresponding sentence in the ransom note. The Christmas letter sentence contained 27 words and three commas while the ransom note sentence had 29 words and two commas. Both the Christmas letter and ransom note sentences have similar structure with the opening clause containing seven and eight words followed by a comma, respectively. However, the Christmas letter utilized a comma before "and hence" while the ransom note did not. Both sentences used "and hence" when the "and" is not necessary. In summation, the word usage and sentence structure was remarkably similar between the ransom note sentence and the 1997 Christmas letter sentence.

In one of Patsy's sections in the Ramsey's book, *The Death of Innocence*, she stated, "Actually, I have no idea why we used that phrase." (Ramsey 2001) Patsy wrote the 1997 Christmas letter, as well as the previous Christmas letters. It was not a collaborative effort, other than she probably talked to family members to gain input. Nevertheless, in the book, Patsy stated she had no idea why "we" used the phrase. She tried to lessen the linkage between the writing and herself. It was subtle, but Patsy tried to deflect the commonalities between her Christmas letter and the ransom note by implying she and John wrote the Christmas letter as a joint effort.

Though there have been some experts who have stated Patsy was not the writer of the ransom note, most of the debate has been over the degree of certainty various experts can place on their conclusions regarding Patsy's authorship of the ransom note. Most experts probably fall short of the criteria of "beyond a reasonable doubt" in their opinions of Patsy's authorship. This is mainly attributable to the alterations in Patsy's writing samples coupled with the concealment tactics in the ransom note. Yet, most hand-writing experts who worked the Ramsey case believed she wrote the ransom note.

Once it has been established that Patsy wrote the ransom note, though maybe not at the highest threshold of confidence, a box can be drawn around the possibilities of what happened on the night of December 25th, 1996. Patsy was not necessarily the killer, but she was intimately involved in the cover-up and would most likely have known the identity of the killer(s). It does not eliminate the possibility of an intruder, even an intruder unknown to the

Ramseys, though it makes the scenario highly improbable.

With a young child found dead in her home, in order to successfully cover-up what actually happened, the ransom note was almost a necessity. There had to be something compelling, pointing toward an intruder. Breaking a window or a door were not viable options in the middle of the night. The ransom note had to be written. However, the one item necessary to convey an intruder is the primary piece of evidence refuting all intruder only theories.

Chapter 8 – Tracing the Note

Since the ransom note is the most critical piece of evidence, it is valuable to plot the location of the note throughout the night and early morning hours. The note did not move by itself, though no fingerprints were found on the note. Identifying the likely location of the ransom note at various points may help to uncover what actually happened.

Before discovery

If Patsy authored the ransom note then the progression of the ransom note requires less work and analysis. At some point after the death of JonBenét, Patsy sat down at the kitchen table, using a pen and pad of paper from the house, and wrote the ransom note. After writing the note, she placed the pen and pad of paper back in their appropriate locations. The ransom note was lain out on a stair rung on the spiral staircase between the first and second floor. After placing the note, Patsy stepped over the note and proceeded back to bed. The note stayed there until Patsy "discovered" it the following morning. The note traveled a straight-forward path.

If an intruder wrote the ransom note, we have a few options for how the note's life evolved. If the intruder wrote the note prior to the murder, he most likely picked up a pen and pad of paper from the kitchen area and wrote it sitting at the kitchen table while the Ramseys were at the White's house. Upon completion, he replaced the pen and paper back in their proper locations. Now he has a three-page incriminating note in his possession. He could have hidden it on the first floor somewhere, but he most likely put it in the basement so it would not be detected by the Ramseys when they returned home later in the evening.

Since the intruder most likely ascended the spiral staircase to abduct JonBenét and then came down the same staircase with her, the ransom note was not on the staircase at that time. The intruder would not have wanted to step over the note carrying a child. And the police demonstrated the extreme difficulty in achieving this task without a child in tow. Based on testing, there was no indication anyone stepped on the ransom note.

As the intruder toured the house learning the layout and location of light switches, the note remained in the basement. It may have been moved once or twice within the basement as the intruder tried to find a better location for safe storage, or it may have stayed in one place. Once the family arrived home and settled in for the night, the intruder left the basement, without the note, to apprehend JonBenét.

At this juncture, it must still be assumed the intruder intended to abduct JonBenét for ransom. Under this scenario, the intruder made an interesting decision by taking her to the basement. He may have gone to the basement to retrieve the ransom note. However, if JonBenét was incapacitated, the intruder had no need to take her with him to the basement. He could have left her by the front or back door while he got the note.

Here is a pivotal point in the intruder theory because there needs to be a determination as to the number of intruders involved. Based on the schizophrenic nature of the crime (molestation, brutality, ransom, and care shown around the body of JonBenét), it appeared to have been perpetrated by more than one individual. If the evening involved more than one intruder, it complicates the various scenarios. Even if there were two intruders, both of them likely went to JonBenét's room to retrieve her. Also, to be able to explain how an actual attempted kidnapping resulted in a murder, there almost had to be two or more intruders. This is the case because we have already established the note was not left on the stairs until after JonBenét was taken from her room. For a legitimate attempted kidnapping to have taken place, the note had to be left on the stairs before JonBenét was killed but after she was taken from her room - a pretty narrow window of time.

For some reason the intruders decided to take JonBenét to the basement prior to removing her from the house. There was some unknown advantage to taking her to the basement. One of the intruders remained with her while the other intruder went upstairs to leave the ransom note on the back staircase. While the second intruder was momentarily upstairs, the first intruder managed to molest, strangle, strike, and kill JonBenét. When the second intruder returned to the basement, he found her dead. In a panic the two intruders left through a small window in the basement, leaving the child and note behind.

Without a second perpetrator, it is not clear how the intruder planned to control JonBenét while he ran upstairs to place the note on the spiral staircase. The plan had to involve either additional conspirators or a means to prevent JonBenét from screaming or escaping. Thus, reinforcing the likelihood the kidnappers would have entered the house with a means to either incapacitate or control her. If so, there is no justification for leaving the body behind.

With regard to the placement of the ransom note, it could imply the intruder knew the routines of the Ramseys, such as the Ramseys use of the back staircase in the morning. The placement of the ransom note is of particular interest because most of the intruder theories believe the intruder left through a basement window. Regardless of when the ransom note was written, it was not placed on the spiral staircase until after JonBenét was taken from her bedroom. When and how did the note get from the basement back up to the first floor (or even from the kitchen onto the spiral staircase)?

Under the first scenario, the note was taken to the first floor while JonBenét remained in the basement, but still alive. For the note to have been left while JonBenét was in the basement alive, it would indicate she was either incapacitated in some manner or an additional intruder was present (one to stay with her while the other placed the note on the spiral staircase). Under this scenario, either something happened to JonBenét while one intruder placed the ransom note upstairs or something happened after his return. Under the scenario of an actual ransom, at this point the intruders would be planning to take JonBenét out of the house. Apparently, they planned to drag her through the basement window, window well, and out into the yard. This would follow the logic and consistency of the theory; otherwise, they would have just taken her out the first floor rather than go to the basement. Something had to have changed in the plan, because the intruders planned to take her out of the house through one of the basement windows, but she was left behind. Panic and confusion were the most plausible reasons for the change in plan. Applying even a small sum of logic, the intruders would have taken JonBenét with them for no other reason than if they disposed of the body it would be harder to determine the killer(s), thus lower the likelihood of capture and subsequent conviction. They chose not to take her.

Under the second scenario, the killer(s) left the ransom note after JonBenét died. Therefore, the ransom note was designed to cover-up what actually happened. There was no evidence of anyone trying to remove the body from the house. Once the killer(s) left the note on the spiral staircase, the killers chose to go back downstairs to leave through a small window in the basement where they would have to climb out, push off a grate, and replace the grate, rather than just walk out a door on the first floor. It is significantly more plausible the killer(s) would have left the house through a back door on the main level rather than go back downstairs to crawl through a tiny window.

After discovery

When Patsy "discovered" the ransom note in the early morning hours of December 26, 1996, she provided conflicting statements regarding what she did with the note. During her official interviews, she indicated she left the note downstairs, and she also stated she had the note with her when she ran to the second floor to look for JonBenét.

John Ramsey's statements were just as confusing. He stated he met Patsy on the second floor as she was running up the stairs. At one point during an official interview, John indicated Patsy handed him the note, but he also stated the note may have been downstairs. He also stated he was not sure when he first saw the note. Neither John nor Patsy committed to the location of the ransom note during their official interviews. Later, when they conferred for their book, *The Death of Innocence*, they somewhat collaborated by saying the note was left downstairs (Ramsey 2001). Both of their statements surrounding the location of the ransom note and checking on Burke were conflicting and confusing. Something about this timeframe was problematic for the Ramseys, but there is nothing specifically identifying the issue(s) they were concealing during this sequence.

Based on the conflicting statements from John and Patsy, both note pathways are analyzed. If Patsy took the note with her upstairs, then she would have possibly crumpled or altered it as she ran up the spiral staircase in a panicked state. There was no indication of such damage. Once John arrived from the third floor, Patsy handed it to him. If John, Patsy, Burke, and the note were all on the second floor, it does not make sense for John to have gone to the first floor to read the note. Though, under this scenario, John would have taken the note to the first floor where he placed it on the hallway floor to read it more closely. No one documented the note's location between the 9-1-1 call and the time the first police officer arrived, but it most likely stayed in the kitchen area. Upon Officer French's arrival, he took the ransom note into police custody.

If Patsy left the note on the spiral staircase, then she would have had to step over it to get upstairs. And John would have had to maneuver over the note on his way down the spiral staircase. No one asked John how he stepped over the note, as the note's location during this timeframe was not clear during any of the interviews. According to the Ramsey's book, once John started reading the note on the first floor he yelled to Patsy asking about Burke's safety. At the time, Patsy paced on the second floor landing. John darted up the spiral staircase, and both he and Patsy checked on Burke. John then descended the main staircase back to the kitchen area where he continued reading the note. As with the previous scenario, it is believed the note stayed in the kitchen area until the police took custody of it.

Tracing the path of the ransom note demonstrates how unlikely it was that an intruder perpetuated the acts against JonBenét. The intruder would have been running up and down the stairs between the basement and the main floor in order to place the note on the spiral staircase. Further, since the note most likely remained in the basement for most of the evening (under an intruder theory), there is no logical course of actions that would lead one to believe an intruder actually intended to receive a ransom.

Chapter 9 – Intruder Theory

Within the investigation, individuals who believed someone outside of the immediate Ramsey family was responsible for the death of JonBenét were said to ascribe to the "intruder theory." There are various items that could indicate one or more intruders were in the Ramsey house on December 25th, 1996. And any theory or concept based on a Ramsey perpetrating the JonBenét murder must successfully refute the intruder theory or show how an intruder(s) conspired with a Ramsey.

Any unaccounted for item has become part of the evidence validating an intruder theory. Combine a completely corrupted crime scene with the sporadic memories of John and Patsy Ramsey, and the list of unidentified items grew throughout the investigation. The Ramsey's memories were most confident and detailed when it validated their innocence, while vague or totally void when it could implicate them. When the Ramseys were shown pictures from inside their house and asked to identify unusual or out of place items, every item they identified has been added to the list of evidence furthering the intruder theory.

Upon entering any house, one would undoubtedly find unexplainable fingerprints or other traces. The Boulder Police Department, who allowed the crime scene to be completely contaminated, has not been able to tie every piece of evidence to a specific individual. This is not surprising, but it does create some doubt. The number of police and other authorized personnel who entered the Ramsey crime scene was substantial. Many people who entered the home had no official role other than curiosity. It is unlikely all of them admitted they entered the house. Therefore, we have a situation where even authorized individuals have a vested interest in not divulging the entire truth regarding their whereabouts in the crime scene.

In a crime scene, every person entering brings something with them, and every person exiting takes something out. At least some of the numerous people who entered the Ramsey house surrounding the death of JonBenét brought DNA-related matter (hair, skin flakes, other genetic material, etc.) into or out of the crime scene. Any number of persons who entered the Ramsey's house could have brought DNA-related matter with them from another person (spouse, child, etc.), also known as "secondary transfer." Within the Ramsey house, secondary transfer and crime scene contamination render much of the DNA evidence questionable at best. The DNA will be analyzed in more detail in Chapter 10.

Fibers are one of the best arguments for one or more intruders. Unlike fingerprints, fibers cannot be linked conclusively to a specific item. Forensic analysis can only reach a confidence level of "consistent with." Therefore, a match of fibers will never be definitive. Intruder theorists can argue any fiber found in or near the crime scene could be linked to anyone or anything. As a result, there will always be doubt, a perfect scenario to ensure the perpetual state of any intruder theory.

Four black and red fibers were found on the duct tape placed over JonBenét's mouth. Based on forensic testing, the fibers were consistent with the jacket Pasty wore on the night of December 25, 1996. At first glance, Patsy's jacket matching fibers on the duct tape was an extremely compelling piece of evidence. The duct tape never left the wine cellar, and Patsy had supposedly not been in the wine cellar on December 26th. Even though Patsy collapsed onto JonBenét's body when she was on the living room floor, John ripped the tape off JonBenét's mouth prior to carrying her to the first floor. This contact would not have facilitated a transfer. It is possible the fibers from Patsy's jacket could have attached to JonBenét, her clothes, or bedding when she put her to bed on December 25th. Based on Patsy's erratic and confusing statements regarding when she wore the jacket, it is not clear whether she wore the jacket or not when she put JonBenét to bed the previous evening. Furthermore, since the fibers cannot be tied conclusively to Patsy's jacket, it could be argued it came from an intruder, a position that can never be definitively proven wrong.

Another example existed with the presence of fibers found around JonBenét's vaginal area, her shirt, as well as on the ligature. Initially, reports indicated the fibers found on JonBenét were consistent with fibers taken from a pillow sham and comforter found in a suitcase in the basement. Other reports have indicated the fibers do not match the items found in the suitcase or any other items found in the house, which would imply an intruder must have removed the item that matched these fibers. However, Pam Paugh, Patsy's sister, removed many items from the house prior to the police conducting a thorough search. The item that matches the fibers in question may have been removed during this visit. According to Steve Thomas, detective on the JonBenét case, the items taken by Ms. Paugh were never cataloged or inventoried in any kind of reliable manner (Thomas

2000). The items removed by Ms. Paugh were lost as evidence.

Two items have been identified as evidence refuting the intruder theory: no footprints in the snow outside the house and spider webs across the grate over the basement window. The lack of footprints in the snow is insignificant. The intruder(s) may have left the house before or while it was still snowing. Not all of the grass was covered with snow and several police officers walked around the Ramsey grounds on the morning of December 26th without leaving footprints in the snow. Therefore, it is certainly plausible someone could have entered and exited the residence without leaving footprints in the snow.

On the morning of December 26, 1996, several police officers noticed the presence of spider webs between the window grate (covering the window to the "train room" in the basement) and the house. The inference was if someone had removed the grate recently there would not be any spider webs present. Experts in the area of spider habits were consulted, and they determined a spider could have spun a web during the early morning hours of the 26th, and based on the sunshine and temperature, it was likely a spider would have re-spun a damaged web. As a result, the presence of spider webs does not indicate no one entered or exited the house through the grate in the preceding hours. Notwithstanding, several Boulder police officers noted the grate over the window looked undisturbed and the debris around the window sill appeared void of movement. The lack of foot prints in the snow may have no evidentiary value, but most of the factors around the basement window indicate it was undisturbed during the previous night.

When developing an intruder theory, there are many avenues from which to select justification. The most obvious is evidence within the crime scene pointing to an outside perpetrator. Another approach is to identify potential external suspects, providing credence to an intruder. One could also look at potential motives. Outside of that, one can look for similar crimes in the area to establish a pattern of behavior. One of the drawbacks to comparing two or more crimes is that one tends to ignore differences while emphasizing similarities. There should be a clear evidentiary link between two crimes in order to convincingly associate them with each other.

In an interesting and scary parallel, there was a young girl who took lessons at Dance West. [JonBenét also took lessons at Dance West at one time.] On September 14, 1997, she was sexually assaulted in her bedroom during the night by an unknown intruder. The girl and her mother had returned home late from a movie that night. According to her mother, she turned on the burglar alarm before going to bed. The girl woke up around midnight and saw a man standing next to her bed. He placed his hand over her mouth. The girl stated the intruder spoke to her by name. The girl's mother heard noise coming from her daughter's room. As she walked into the room the man pushed her aside and left, jumping out of a second floor window.

At this time, there has been no connection between the home invasion/sexual assault on the young girl from Dance West and the JonBenét murder. The similarities, however, are alarming. Though, when one discards dissimilar events, and only focuses on similar events, it is easier to bolster a given theory or perspective. There have been no other murders or kidnappings in and around Boulder, Colorado bearing similarities to the JonBenét Ramsey murder. It does not bode well for the theory of a maniac child molester/murderer on the loose when something of this nature has not occurred in the last 15+ years. Based on the DA's soft approach to crime, even if the perpetrator had been convicted of an unrelated crime he would not have been in prison for the entire 15+ years.

The Ramseys cast suspicion upon numerous individuals, both known and unknown to them. An accusation they were appalled to have leveled against them; however, they asserted it against several friends and acquaintances with little or no supporting evidence. At times, the Ramseys cast suspicion on someone based on almost nothing. For example, John Ramsey told investigators Priscilla White may own a stun gun because she once lived in California. This is not a passing comment he made to a friend during a private conversation. This is a statement he made during an official interview with the District Attorney's Office, regarding the use of a stun gun to immobilize JonBenét prior to her death. John implied Ms. White could be involved in the death of his daughter. John based his theory on the fact Ms. White once lived in California, the most populated state.

The Ramseys have tremendous motivation to identify and alert the authorities to unusual items within their house. It could help the authorities with the investigation, but it also diverted attention away from the Ramseys. Though it is not definitive whether or not the Ramseys provided a list of persons who were in the house and basement to the authorities, they could have left someone out, either intentionally or unintentionally. As a result, the intruder theory could potentially live on forever, since any evidence linked to an unlisted (unidentified) person would never be cleared.

There were no signs of forced entry at the Ramsey residence on the morning of December 26, 1996. According to the police, the entire house was locked on the morning of the 26th. John Ramsey told the police all the doors and windows were locked when he checked the house. Nevertheless, John Fernie indicated he found the butler door unlocked when he arrived shortly after 6:00 a.m. on the morning of the 26th. Most likely both John Ramsey and the police checked the butler door after John Fernie entered the premise, thus it was locked at that time. An unlocked door, however, provided a portal for an intruder to enter and/or exit the house unimpeded.

As a platform for the intruder theory, there are various unexplained items or unknown factors within the crime. Almost every intruder theory utilizes one or more of the unaccounted for items as proof of an intruder. Each one will be discussed individually to assess its impact on determining what actually happened.

Footprint, with the letters "Hi Tec" - An unaccounted for footprint with the letters, "Hi-Tec" was found in the concrete dust in the wine cellar. Investigators have been unable to connect it to anyone. No one has a firm list of who entered the basement before or after the murder. Even if one of the Ramsey's had a boot with this sole, it would be contingent on the Ramseys turning it into the investigators. It took the Ramseys over a year to turn over the clothes they wore on the night/morning of JonBenét's murder.

Though there is nothing indicating John Fernie entered in the basement on the morning of December 26th, he claimed in 1998 that the police had still not noted the type of shoes he wore on that day. It is quite probable there are many other known individuals whose shoes have not been accounted for by the police. Due to the less than thorough investigation coupled with the overall crime scene contamination, this unaccounted for piece of evidence provides almost no insight into the possibility of an intruder.

Palm print – The police found an unidentified palm print on the door to the wine cellar. Investigators were unable to identify the source. It was originally reported the print did not belong to one of the Ramseys. Subsequently, newspaper reports indicated the print belonged to Melinda Ramsey, a daughter of John Ramsey from his first marriage.

It was unlikely an intruder left a print, since any intruder(s) most likely utilized gloves or similar mechanism while inside the house. No other confirmed, unidentified fingerprints were found in the crime scene. As a result, a palm print would only have resulted from the removal of one of the gloves. Since no other unaccounted for fingerprints were found at the crime scene, it is highly unlikely this print pertained to the crimes committed. Regardless, the palm print presented another piece of evidence pointing toward an intruder until it was proven false.

Pubic hair – During a search, the police discovered a pubic hair on the blanket wrapped around JonBenét. It was originally reported the hair did not belong to John, Patsy, or Burke Ramsey. The unaccounted pubic hair found within the wine cellar presented a viable connection to the crime. Even the extensive contamination of the crime scene would unlikely result in an unknown pubic hair. However, according to James Kolar in *Foreign Faction*, DNA tests indicate it was not a pubic hair, and it could have come from Patsy Ramsey or another person on her maternal side of the family (Kolar 2012).

Scuff mark on wall – The police identified a scuff mark on the basement wall below the window in question. A mark on a basement wall in a house over half a century old is hardly unusual. The scuff on the wall could have been from anything and could have happened at any time, including years before the murder of JonBenét. The basement was rarely cleaned. John and Patsy rarely visited the basement and were completely unfamiliar with the contents or condition of the basement. There is no indication the scuff mark was connected to the death of JonBenét.

Rope - Upon finding JonBenét, John Ramsey found rope wrapped around her neck and wrists. There was no other identical rope found in the Ramsey house. Therefore, the intruder must have brought and removed the rope from the house. The rope was small and not the most effective tool for restraining, even a child. Both John Andrew and Burke Ramsey had similar rope though it apparently did not match. The origin of the rope is unknown. Though, there is nothing to suggest the rope used on JonBenét was not *all* the rope. The rope was used in conjunction with the garrote, though the garrote came from the house. Without the accompanying use of the garrote, the failure to find the rope's origin would be much more conclusive of an intruder's presence. It could have been argued the intruder(s) brought in and removed the weapons used to kill JonBenét. However, the garrote, conveniently located near the crime scene, was used with the rope to help facilitate the murder. Without the garrote, the rope's effectiveness was significantly reduced.

Unlike fingerprints, a piece of rope cannot be conclusively tied to another piece of rope. The two pieces can be highly consistent, but most analysis does not reach the level of a match. Even still, according to information gleaned from the investigation, the police found no other rope consistent with the rope found wrapped around JonBenét. It is still an unknown.

Duct tape – The perpetrator placed duct tape over JonBenét's mouth after she was either dead or unconscious. It was most likely part of the cover-up, not the actual murder. The duct tape served no real purpose. The duct tape was similar to common household tape. It could have been purchased at a local hardware store. The Ramseys never provided all of their receipts or credit card statements to the authorities; therefore, there is no way to verify if the Ramsey's purchased it (or the rope).

The duct tape was unnecessary to the crime. If the perpetrator incapacitated JonBenét then there would have been no need to duct tape her mouth. There was no tongue depression on the tape, which would have been expected with a conscious victim. Most victims would try to push the duct tape away from his/her mouth. There was no indication she was ever conscious while the tape was over her mouth.

There are many possible elements of varying certainty pointing toward an intruder; however, the missing roll of duct tape poses a moderate likelihood either an intruder or one of the Ramseys left the house on the night of the 25th. The police never found the duct tape roll. It is possible it could have been thrown into a nearby trash can, where it would have avoided detection. It also could have been thrown in a trash can in the Ramsey house, whereby it was discarded before the police conducted a thorough search. Moreover, Pam Paugh, Patsy Ramsey's sister, could have removed the duct tape and/or rope during her trip to the Ramsey house when she took numerous unaccounted for items in preparation for the funeral.

Unless an intruder had a duffle bag, carrying a roll of duct tape into and out of the house would only be logical if the other criminal elements came from outside the house, though most of the items came from within the house. Further, it would only make sense to bring duct tape if it was a pivotal component of the crime. It was not. The tape was utilized as part of the staging, and it was most likely an after-thought. Notwithstanding, the absence of the duct roll remains an outstanding item.

DNA evidence - The DNA evidence is one of the most compelling, yet also least reliable evidence pointing toward an intruder(s). Though there are many explanations for how unaccounted for DNA could be present on and around JonBenét, it also represents viable evidence of an unknown person(s).

Overall, the familiarity of the crime points inside the house, not outside. Most of the items inventoried as part of evidence collection can be traced back to the inside of the house. Here is a list of the key elements used during or after the murder of JonBenét, coupled with their respective origin:

- Ransom note & pad of paper – Came from inside the house

- Pen used to write the ransom note – Came from inside the house

- Garrote – Came from inside the house

- Rope used to strangle JonBenét – Could not determine its origin (Burke Ramsey and John Andrew Ramsey both had rope.)

- Duct tape - Could not determine its origin, but it may have come from inside the house. Police found similar tape on the back of pictures in JonBenét's bedroom, and a Ramsey receipt from a local hardware store matched the cost of similar duct tape. At this time, there is no conclusive evidence it came from inside the house.

- Baseball bat – Came from inside the house (It was not determined whether it was part of the crime or not.)

- Flashlight – Most likely came from inside the house, though not definitive (It was not determined whether it was part of the crime or not.)

- White blanket found on wine cellar floor – Came from inside the house (JonBenét's bed)

- Barbie nightgown found in wine cellar – Came from inside the house (JonBenét's nightgown)

- Broken window in basement – John Ramsey broke the window during the late summer or early fall of 1996.

- Suitcase – Came from inside the house (John Andrew utilized it.)

Almost all of the items used to perpetuate the murder of JonBenét and subsequent cover-up can be definitively tied to the Ramsey house. The items not tied to the house are common household items. The elements of the crime point toward a person familiar with the household, not a stranger.

Though the Ramseys and their legal team pushed various disjointed intruder theories, their obvious self-interest mitigated the worthiness of their theories. When Lou Smit, detective for the Boulder District Attorney's Office, entered the scene and began pushing the possibility of an intruder it started to take hold. Mr. Smit is the father of most aspects of the current intruder theory. He provided a much needed devil's advocate role to the media and Boulder Police Department. Many of the points he made needed to be analyzed and either refuted or confirmed.

Detective Lou Smit introduced the possibility of a stun gun into the investigation based on autopsy pictures. Mr. Smit speculated several marks on JonBenét could have been the result of a stun gun. Under the premise, an intruder used a stun gun to disable JonBenét in her room and then carried her limp body to the basement.

Many reasons make the use of a stun gun to immobilize JonBenét implausible: 1) Stun guns can produce a crackling noise or a loud popping noise, which John and Patsy would have likely heard. 2) The use of a stun gun could cause the victim to scream out in pain, especially a small child. 3) Stun guns provide significant variability in the time it takes to disable a victim, which can range from several seconds up to minutes. The Air Taser model reported by Lou Smit as the one most likely used, has also been reported to not cause victims to go unconscious. It does not produce consistent results when disabling a victim, thus significantly reducing its worthiness as a means to control a victim.

If one accepts the use of a stun gun, the likely theory points toward a stranger because if it were someone who knew her then he would not have to disable her. This theory contradicts most intruder theories, which presume the murderer(s) knew JonBenét; therefore, the stun gun would not have been necessary. It could have been used as a sexual torture device, and then it would no longer exclude persons who knew JonBenét. Yet, there is no compelling reason to believe a stun gun was utilized in the murder.

Detectives discovered a brochure for stun guns in the Ramsey house, but both John and Patsy claimed to have never looked at it or purchased a stun gun. When asked, the Ramseys claimed to be completely ignorant of stun guns. The concept of a stun gun as an instrument to carry out the JonBenét murder pointed directly toward a stranger. A family member would not have to subdue her. With the discovery of the stun gun brochure in the Ramsey house, the suspicion turned back toward them. No stun gun was found in the house or connected to the Ramseys in any way. The Ramseys may have owned a stun gun, but no evidence has been found to substantiate this claim. Furthermore, without exhuming her body, there is no compelling indication anyone used a stun gun on JonBenét.

Mr. Smit also introduced the basement window as likely entrance or exit portal for an intruder. The emphasis on the basement window re-ignited or initiated John Ramsey's concerns surrounding the basement window. According to Fleet White, when he and John came upon the broken window on the afternoon of December 26th, John told Fleet he had broken the window the proceeding summer. In John's April 1997 interview with the police, he told the investigators there was no glass around the window in the basement, thus indicating it was not a fresh break.

John told investigators in June of 1998, "It was terribly unusual for me [window open]." During his interview with Barbara Walters in March of 2000, John responded he "...was a bit alarmed [with the window being open]..." At other times John conceded the window was open periodically because it was hot in the basement. According to John, he found the window only open a crack, but he closed it before anyone could verify it was open or check for fingerprints. He demonstrated concern regarding the Samsonite suitcase placed below the window. Though John acknowledged he seldom went down to the basement, he feigned familiarity with the normal condition of the basement.

On the main floor of the Ramsey house, there were six doors and around 30 windows, which provided viable options for gaining access to the house. Entering through the grate would have required the intruder to remove the grate and climb through a small window. An intruder would have had to replace the grate in order to cover his tracks while he remained inside the house. The suspicious act of climbing into the house through a window grate could draw attention from neighbors. It would have also been one of the most difficult methods for exiting the house. Not to mention, removing a child through the window grate would be extremely difficult and an unlikely means of exit. Further, as noted in an earlier chapter, by tracing the possible path and locations of the ransom note, there is no reason for an intruder to have left the note on the spiral staircase to the second floor and then leave the house by way of the basement window.

There has been much discussion about the suitcase found underneath the basement window with a grate.

Though, according to Detective Steve Thomas, Fleet White acknowledged he moved the suitcase on the morning of December 26, 1996 (Thomas 2000). Fleet indicated he moved the suitcase to look for broken glass, which he did not find.

After committing a murder and "botched kidnapping," why would one or more individuals leave through the downstairs window during the middle of the night? One could have easily walked out one of the many doors. He would have to crawl through a window, lift the grate, climb out of the window well, and then replace the grate. This is an unlikely scenario.

During John Ramsey's official June 1998 interviews, he stated the glass found on the floor in front of the basement window was not enough to indicate a new break of the window. John also stated when he went to the basement on the morning of December 26th there was a chair in front of the doorway leading into the train room. For someone to have left through the room he would have had to pull the chair into the doorway upon entering the room. There was no reason for an intruder try to conceal his exit through a broken window. According to John, the window in question was also only open about one inch when he found it on the morning of December 26th, which would indicate the intruder(s) reached back and pulled the window partially shut after exiting through the window. Though John may want to believe one or more intruders left through the basement window, there is little information supporting this theory and the plausibility is questionable. If one or more intruders did enter the Ramsey house on December 25, 1996, it is highly unlikely they entered or exited through the window in the basement or utilized a stun gun.

According to Patsy Ramsey's statements, JonBenét's bedroom door was in the same position on the morning of December 26th as it was the night before when she put her to bed. The door was only open a few inches. This would indicate the person who removed JonBenét from her bedroom either had someone with him to close the door behind them or he pulled the door shut while carrying JonBenét. This is achievable, but unlikely.

The introduction of an intruder only extends the circle of suspicion beyond the immediate Ramsey family to other family members and close friends. There is too much familiarity within the crime to lean toward a stranger. And most elements of the crime point to more than one individual, coupled with the discovery of multiple, unidentified DNA profiles. As a result, if one believes the DNA evidence, the intruder theory would have to include at least two unknown individuals. However, if one discounts the DNA evidence the intruder theory would only have to include one intruder. Under both intruder scenarios, the possibility of Ramsey involvement still exists.

One perplexing component regarding a theory involving one or more of the Ramseys is a lack of motive. Needless to say, there is no clear motive for an intruder to kill JonBenét either. Many motives have been bantered about throughout the investigation, to include: kidnapping, molestation, revenge, home invasion, or some combination thereof. None of these motives required them to kill JonBenét. There was nothing about the crime that showed premeditation or planning. Every element of the crime was an opportunistic endeavor. The stick used to create the garrote happened to be right next to where JonBenét was likely murdered. The paper and pen for the ransom note were in the kitchen. Even the mysterious pineapple was on the kitchen table.

Contrary to Patsy's statements on *20/20* in March of 2000, there is no definitive reason to believe the crime was premeditated. Nothing within the crime exudes any level of planning or even organization.

Based on the circumstances of the crime, premeditation can be ruled out. The acts were impulsive, not planned. Of the motives listed above, kidnapping can be removed as it requires a plan. It is hard to conceive of kidnapping someone without a plan. Revenge can be impulsive, especially when it is driven by rage. However, the long, drawn out nature of the crime does not support that theory. There is absolutely nothing about the crime that would convey revenge.

Sexual molestation could certainly result on impulse. Sexual predators may often act on impulse or claim they have desires that cannot be controlled. The impulse was not tied to opportunity, unless the individual was already in the house or near the house with knowledge of JonBenét's imminent presence. There are many elements of the crime that lean toward sexual molestation as the primary motive behind the crime, but not by an unknown intruder.

John found JonBenét wearing her underwear. It was later determined she had been sexually molested. She could have been molested to some extent while still wearing her underwear, but most likely the perpetrator pulled down her underwear as he molested her. Therefore, someone pulled up JonBenét's underwear after-the-fact. The underwear was likely pulled up as part of the cover-up. The cover-up was most likely conducted by someone other than the perpetrator of the murder, thus conveying the schizophrenic dynamic of the crime.

During John's official April 1997 interviews, he referred to the white blanket found in the wine cellar as "...kind of folded around her legs." Over a year later, during his June 1998 interviews, he described the blanket as being "...caught up around and crossed in front of her as if somebody was tucking her in...someone had put her there comfortably...to keep her warm." John was referring to a blanket kept on JonBenét's bed though it is not known whether it was on her bed the night she died. Either way, there are few logical scenarios for how the blanket ended up in the basement wine cellar. Most have postulated someone brought the blanket to the basement after her death to comfort her to some extent. Under such a theory, the implication is that someone very close to her was involved in the murder and/or cover-up. It would have been someone who would want her to be comfortable, even in death.

Another possible theory contends the blanket was either carried by JonBenét on her decent to the basement or the intruder(s) carried it with him to use during the molestation. Most intruder theories believe she was incapacitated prior to leaving her bedroom; otherwise, she would have undoubtedly screamed out. As a result, JonBenét most likely did not carry the blanket. The molestation in the basement was most likely considered an impulsive decision. Under this scenario, the intruder(s) would not have grabbed the blanket as an instrument to facilitate molestation.

Other than the likely scenario where an individual very close to JonBenét brought the blanket to comfort her, another possibility is the blanket was caught up in JonBenét's pajamas in some manner, which resulted in the blanket attaching to her for the trip to the basement cellar. If the white blanket was either in the dryer or a closet, then the only reasonable option was for someone with intimate knowledge of the household to have taken it to the basement.

Upon initial review, many people are viable suspects. This is predicated on the belief an intruder was involved in the crime. Almost all factions (excluding "small foreign factions") of the JonBenét investigation believe the person or persons who committed this act had intimate knowledge of the family, or at the very least, were acquainted with the family. Therefore, since almost everyone surrounding the family has been investigated and cleared it does not bode well for the belief a person(s) close to, but outside of the Ramseys committed the murder. There are many people outside of the immediate Ramsey family who have been interviewed as potential suspects. Some of the individuals align more closely with the murder than others, but all have been cleared.

Based on the DNA evidence, there were at least two unknown perpetrators inside the Ramsey home on the night of December 25, 1996. To complete the murder and cover-up, the perpetrators would have left their place of residence sometime between 4:00 p.m. and 7:00 p.m. on Christmas day, assuming a short commute and no preparation was required prior to arriving at the Ramsey's house. Though an exact time could not be determined, JonBenét most likely died sometime between 11:00 p.m. on December 25th and 2:00 a.m. on December 26th, 1996. Assuming the perpetrators did not have to dump any evidence or conduct any other post-murder activities, they would have returned home between 11:30 p.m. and 2:30 a.m. As a result, the perpetrators were gone somewhere between four and a half and ten and a half hours during Christmas day and night. This requires a substantial alibi to be able to account for this sizable timeframe, especially since the alibi could not rely on anyone else to substantiate. The only plausible options would be for the perpetrators to be loners (though working together in this instance) who did not have to account for their time to anyone. However, this leaves them without a verifiable alibi, unless the perpetrators provided each other with alibis. The sheer time necessary to complete the murder makes it difficult for someone to accomplish this crime without being missed by someone. Furthermore, the crime occurred on Christmas night, a time when there were limited alibi possibilities.

From the evidence, it does not appear the perpetrators of JonBenét's murder had a plan. There is no compelling reason why intruders would have entered the house hours before they needed to be there. There was no overarching purpose. If the murder, kidnapping, and/or molestation took place in the middle of the night there was no reason to arrive in the late afternoon/early evening hours. Possible partial explanations have included: to understand the floor plan of the house and to write the ransom note. Though, neither or both of these actions justify breaking into the Ramsey house hours earlier than necessary. Every minute in the house would expose the perpetrator to being caught. Minutes would feel like hours as the impending additional felonies would weigh on the conscious of the intruder. Even criminally insane perpetrators conceal their crimes and do not traditionally take excess risks.

To turn the argument back on the intruder theorists, one must generate a reasonable explanation for why a perpetrator would enter the Ramsey house multiple hours before it was necessary. There is a significantly higher risk of getting caught. There was no real benefit to entering the house early and under many proposed intruder theories, the crime was premeditated. It is not clear whether the kidnapping or murder was supposed to be premeditated. There was no compelling reason for one or more perpetrators to commit home invasion and then lay and wait.

If the intruder(s) broke into the house while the Ramseys were at the White's house then he would have entered the house in the daylight or early evening hours. He would have walked around the outside of the house, in areas where people would not normally be present, except children playing. Not only would he have had to climb into the window well and through a window, but he would have replaced the grate. The grate needed to be replaced because the intruders needed to stay in the house for several hours.

There is some evidence indicating one or more intruders were present in the Ramsey house. Of the list of evidence pointing toward an intruder, the most perplexing is the duct tape. The duct tape was utilized as part of the cover-up, yet the roll cannot be found. The other examples of intruder proof were most likely a result of crime scene contamination or other explainable factors. As a result, when all of the evidence and inputs are analyzed the probability of an intruder's presence during the night of December 25, 1996 does not pass the test of "more likely than not." As has been identified prior, even the presence of an intruder on that night does not conclusively eliminate the Ramseys involvement in the murder and/or cover-up.

The ransom note is the strongest evidence against an unknown intruder breaking into the Ramsey house with the primary objective of molesting JonBenét. An unknown intruder does not have to explain his presence. A ransom note would result in extensive, additional evidence left behind. There was no obvious benefit for an intruder to write a ransom note. A contrived explanation could be guilt. The intruder suffered from tremendous guilt in killing the little girl. He had to convince himself kidnapping was the motive and the murder was an accident. If guilt motivated the writing of the ransom note then the intruder would have written a letter stating it was an accident. He did not mean for anything to happen, including the molestation. Instead, the intruder wrote a dissertation that conveyed extreme familiarity and tons of details pertaining to a made-up kidnapping, versus washing his guilt. The threats and vicious nature of the note did not construe a consolatory tone. Nothing in the note indicated it was written to alleviate guilt.

As with most aspects of any intruder theory, any extrapolation of what happened or how it could have happened, generates an intruder(s) extremely familiar with the Ramsey family. It would have been someone very familiar with the household and someone with whom JonBenét felt comfortable. All of the individuals who fit this profile have been eliminated as suspects.

Chapter 10 – The Black Swan

Nassim Nicholas Taleb developed the theory of the black swan. The concept states that to an observer a given event is not expected or it is a surprise, coupled with the event having a major impact. Normal modeling within financial, technological, or scientific arenas is not able to account for the high impact combined with the fact the event is more likely to occur than the underlying statistics would indicate (Taleb 2007). In the JonBenét murder investigation, the black swan is the touch DNA found on and around JonBenét.

Few would expect to find unknown DNA on and around JonBenét's body, if there were no intruder, though it is probably fairly likely. The impact of the touch DNA is significant. The unknown DNA is believed to have kept the grand jury from indicting Patsy Ramsey. At this point, the forensic analysis has not identified the sources of all of the touch DNA from the crime scene.

In many criminal cases, DNA evidence is used to determine whether someone was at a given location, usually the crime scene. In cases where the individual denied he was at the crime scene, finding his DNA there provides near bulletproof evidence of his presence. Utilizing DNA collection in this manner makes it highly unlikely contamination could generate the presence of a specific individual's DNA at a crime scene, though human error could be a factor. DNA evidence is the most useful when investigators have a specific suspect and the suspect is not known to the victim. In general, DNA use in this situation proves *extremely* accurate.

DNA use in other circumstances generates reliable results, but a lower level of confidence. For example, the JonBenét Ramsey investigators used DNA evidence to eliminate suspects. If a given suspect does not match the found DNA, then he/she was deemed not involved in the crime. The DNA has also been referenced as additional evidence of an intruder. With the implications of the DNA, it is imperative investigators determine the source of the unaccounted for DNA.

If one embraces the presence of one or more intruders, the absence of unaccounted for fingerprints throughout the house has led most to believe the intruder(s) wore gloves. There were no unknown fingerprints on the ransom note, corresponding pen, or on the bowl of pineapple. The police did not find any unidentified fingerprints on any door knobs, windows, or walls. The touch DNA would indicate the perpetrators were not wearing gloves, hence the ability to leave the miniscule DNA. If an intruder wore gloves and most likely winter clothes, what part of the intruder(s) generated the touch DNA?

It is an extremely difficult task to account for all DNA found in a given location. For example, assume a murder took place in the men's locker room of a local gym. A men's gym locker room is loaded with various DNA, fingerprints, and hair follicles. Could an investigator conclusively account for all the hair or DNA found in the locker room? This is a semi-public location with a large number of people coming and going. Most of the individuals who have passed-through the locker room would most likely be male members, employees, maintenance personnel, and cleaning persons. Though it would be time-consuming, one could take DNA, hair, and fingerprint samples from all of those parties.

For the sake of simplicity, we will just focus on hair. An investigator obtains hair samples from all male members and authorized employees. It is possible one of the people in the locker room may have brought a hair into the locker room not of his own person, a secondary transference. Therefore, all of the persons on the list need to identify all family members and others they may have come into close contact with recently. This would provide a comprehensive list of potential matches.

What if one of the members is having an affair? It is unlikely he listed his mistress as someone whose hair could have made its way into the locker room. As a result, someone would lie to the authorities for a reason completely unrelated to the investigation at hand. Other innocent possibilities could lead to an individual being overlooked, such as an error in the gym's computer system, poor company records, or a memory lapse by an employee. Therefore, it would be extremely difficult to confidently account for all of the hair within a locker room.

The inability to account for all collected hair does not indicate an unknown individual entered the locker room. The unidentified hair could be due to secondary transference (unnamed member's mistress). Notwithstanding, it does not exclude the possibility of an unknown perpetrator engaged in malice; it just demonstrates there are other possibilities as well.

In the Ramsey house, the number of individuals who entered the house was far less than the above example, but the same principles apply. One or two unaccounted for persons could result in the inability to account for DNA present at the crime scene. Add to this, the contamination and chaos of the Ramsey crime scene and unaccounted for DNA was undoubtedly present.

If the coroner found skin or blood under JonBenét's fingernails or another similar set of circumstances, then the DNA would indicate something beyond a mere touch. Information has been released indicating at least two unidentified profiles of DNA have been found at the crime scene. Every additional unmatched DNA profile found at the crime scene lowers the credibility and viability of the already found DNA. What if the DNA evidence indicated five or six unidentified persons? According to James Kolar in *Foreign Faction*, six unidentified DNA strands have been cataloged (Kolar 2012). It is inconceivable a large group perpetrated the botched kidnapping, murder, and cover-up. Though it is already in question, finding additional unmatched DNA would validate that the sensitivity levels of the touch DNA detected irrelevant source material

The statistics around the accuracy of DNA evidence within criminal investigations are almost above reproach. In court cases, attorneys have mentioned the error rate of DNA analysis as one in a billion or more. This is often referred to as "prosecutor's fallacy" because the possibility of error is much higher than the conventional statistics convey because of human error. Additionally, the proven error rate of DNA analysis is considerably higher than purported since false convictions based on DNA evidence have already been established.

There has been some, but limited analysis on DNA presence and transference outside of crime scenes. In one study, the probability of successfully obtaining an adequate profile from someone who touched a given surface varied from 9 – 36%. Of the samples analyzed, approximately 10% contained a secondary transfer. The study noted secondary transfer did occur, but primary transfer was more likely (Daly 2012).

Touch DNA may be so sensitive it will inevitably pick up DNA matter from unlikely sources. If so, touch DNA analysis may be the end of "beyond a reasonable doubt." Depending on the circumstances, unidentifiable DNA at any crime scene could lead to "not guilty" verdicts in many cases where it may be completely irrelevant to the crime. Prosecuting attorneys will have to explain why and how there is unknown DNA at the crime scene. Defense teams could ostensibly hire forensic experts to scour crime scenes in search of unsourced DNA. They would only have to find one sample.

When analyzing the accuracy and reliability of DNA use in a criminal investigation or prosecution, contamination is the largest concern. In general, the more people present at a crime scene, the more likely the evidence or scene has been contaminated. At the Ramsey house, the police failed to properly secure the crime scene. Individuals who were not critical to the crime scene entered and exited the house throughout the early hours of the investigation. No one accurately accounted for all of the persons present or their movements or activities. Items within the house were moved and removed without precise documentation.

The body was touched by at least John Ramsey, Fleet White, Detective Linda Arndt, and Patsy Ramsey. John Ramsey loosened the rope around JonBenét's wrist, tore off the tape over her mouth, and carried her upstairs. Detective Arndt moved JonBenét and placed a blanket over her body, and adjusted the blanket at least once. Someone (not identified) else placed a sweatshirt over JonBenét's exposed feet. Patsy Ramsey lied across JonBenét. All of these activities significantly increased the potential for contamination within the collected DNA. Any DNA findings in this case have to be weighed against the significant contamination at the crime scene.

Another concern within the investigation is the possibility individuals were lying to the authorities for reasons other than involvement in the murder of JonBenét. One or more individuals could be withholding information regarding someone's presence in the Ramsey house, which had nothing to do with JonBenét's death. Someone may have also made a mistake in his recollection of events. Documentation or other recording errors could have occurred during the investigation. In total, the condition of the crime scene, coupled with the surrounding procedural errors, have materially compromised the DNA evidence collected and cast doubt on the reliability of such. The verifiable accuracy of touch DNA pulled from the Ramsey crime scene is weak and unreliable.

Just as with the police, the coroner's office had limited recent experience with murder investigations. Using the same clippers on each finger nail or how the body was handled and secured could have caused irreparable harm to the evidence collected. Cross contamination is probable. Touch DNA could have easily been transferred from one piece of evidence to another by crime scene technicians. An unsecured crime scene further weakens the accuracy of touch DNA testing and reduces its benefit considerably. Errors in the gathering of DNA evidence could have resulted in DNA transferring from one location to the next, thus explaining how the same DNA could be in multiple locations.

In the now famous "Phantom of Heilbronn" case, DNA evidence found at numerous crime scenes (40) tied six murders and other felonies together. The crimes spanned from 1993 to 2009 and covered Austria, France, and Germany. Based on the same DNA identified at all of the crime scenes, investigators connected the crimes and believed they were perpetrated by one individual. According to the DNA analysis, it was a woman.

In March of 2009, investigators came to the conclusion the "Phantom" did not exist. The DNA found at the crime scenes was already present on the cotton swabs used to recover the DNA. The DNA found during the investigations was from contamination during the manufacturing and assembly processing of the cotton swabs. Other cotton swabs were tested before shipping from the same factory, and they contained the same DNA as the crime scenes. All of the swabs used for the various crime scenes were produced by the same factory

Contrary to the excessively transparent approach the Boulder DA's Office and police department had during the early phase of the JonBenét murder investigation, limited information has been released about recent investigative progress or lack thereof. The information released on the DNA analysis has not provided a comprehensive explanation of the approach or results of the various tests. As a result, there is not a complete understanding of the various techniques.

Some of the analysis conducted was on partial DNA profiles. Partial profiles demonstrate a deficiency in the collected sample. In a partial profile, DNA molecules are not present and there is no way to determine what the complete profile is. Contaminated DNA will usually present itself as a partial profile, which means contamination is more likely with a partial profile than a complete profile. Partial profiles can result in false inclusions and false exclusions.

At least some of the foreign DNA analyzed was discovered in JonBenét's underwear. Initially, many investigators believed this had to be the DNA of a perpetrator. However, miniscule foreign DNA could be in her underwear from a bicycle seat or even from the factory where the underwear was made. To follow-up on this hypothesis, investigators obtained unopened packages of underwear manufactured in the same plant in Southeast Asia. Testing of the control samples found human DNA on some of the underwear, thus producing a viable alternative explanation for the presence of unknown DNA.

Some of the DNA tested from various locations on JonBenét was fragmented and did not yield the necessary markers. People who worked at one of the labs where DNA in the JonBenét investigation was tested have said the DNA amount analyzed was so minute it could be incidental to the crime. Some of the DNA analyzed is considered "old DNA," which means it was most likely deposited well before her murder.

There are many issues with the use of DNA evidence in the Ramsey murder investigation. The most damaging factor is the DNA may not be reliable; therefore, all use is flawed. No one (except those involved) knows how many people were involved in the commission of the crime. As a result, a perpetrator involved in the crime could be compared against DNA, which is either contaminated, unrelated to the crime, or from another perpetrator, thus leading investigators to believe he was not involved. It is possible the murderer of JonBenét may not have left enough DNA at the crime scene to determine a match. Therefore, the killer could be eliminated merely because he does not tie to the discovered DNA. Each of the scenarios could lead investigators away from a viable suspect. The use of flawed DNA will cause more harm to the case than good.

The DNA may not match for many reasons, such as contamination, or the depositing of the DNA was unrelated to the crime itself. If the DNA was deposited, for example, in the underwear during manufacturing, the DNA will never tie to anyone, but will still provide reasonable doubt to any other indicted individual. Using DNA as a means to identify a perpetrator(s) when family members were primarily suspected will never present a problem for the family, but will always cause doubt in their guilt.

Due to the failure of the Boulder Police Department to properly secure the crime scene, coupled with other failed procedures, DNA evidence pulled from the Ramsey house has to be viewed skeptically. The opportunity and likelihood of contamination are high. Add to the situation, highly sensitive touch DNA is even more prone to false or misleading conclusions. The DNA's evidentiary value is questionable. It will continue to mislead and confuse investigators. It will allow investigators to clear suspects who may be involved.

Chapter 11 – Family Dynamics

The inter-workings of any relationship are difficult to discern from outside the relationship. The relationships within the Ramsey family are no different. Though both John and Patsy Ramsey described their relationship as very close, most observers disagree with their assessment. A former Ramsey house-keeper described the interaction between John and Patsy as similar to business associates. Many of John and Patsy's interview answers indicate they shared little with each other. In his June 1998 interviews, John stated he and Patsy never discussed JonBenét's bedwetting, and she never mentioned to him that JonBenét had gone to the doctor on three occasions for urinary-related medical problems. Patsy stated she and John never discussed the bowl of pineapple, which was a pretty critical piece of evidence surrounding the murder of their daughter. Numerous other answers to interview questions demonstrated they failed to share their most basic thoughts and feelings with each other.

As previously discussed, John broke the basement window in the late summer of 1996. He broke the window because he did not have his key and Patsy and the children were out of town when he arrived home from a business trip. It was not the first time he had broken the window, as he had lost or forgotten his house key on other occasions. However, Patsy had given their neighbors, the Barnhills, a key to the house. Based on subsequent interview responses, Patsy may have never conveyed this information to John.

During Patsy Ramsey's April 1997 interviews, she stated John did not discuss business matters with her, even if there were problems at work. She stated John handled all the family finances, and she was not aware of his salary or 1996 bonus. Patsy provided a clear line of division between their personal relationship and John's professional career. She expressed no interest in or knowledge of his work, though he worked long hours and was away from home a lot due to his job.

In the Ramsey's 1995 Christmas letter, written by Patsy, she discussed John's business successes. She provided details about John's business beyond the traditional highlights. Patsy identified office locations in Europe and other international expansions. Patsy provided significantly more detail than would be expected from a woman who indicated to the police she was completely unaware of details regarding John's business. It is not clear how Patsy would have known this business information if she was completely removed from the business and never discussed it with John. Patsy may have downplayed her knowledge of the John's business dealings in order to present things in a manner more to her choosing.

Both John and Patsy indicated they never fought or had disagreements. Patsy stated in her official June 1998 interviews she did not "...really know his [John's] habits." The question regarding habits pertained more to his sleep habits, but her response indicated a more open-ended answer. Patsy stated she could not speak to John's normal habits or activities, which conveyed a distant relationship. Patsy was quite adamant as to the closeness she and John shared, yet most of her responses about their relationship demonstrated the opposite was true. She did not discuss JonBenét's well-being with John. Patsy most likely never discussed Burke's health with John either, but the interviewers never asked her about it.

During his official June 1998 interviews, John dismissed JonBenét's bed-wetting problem. He regarded it as a part of childhood and not a problem. Most of his answers indicate he was unaware of how often JonBenét wet the bed. In Patsy's official April 1997 interviews, she stated she was not sure if John knew about JonBenét's bed-wetting. Moreover, John was completely unaware of when JonBenét went to the doctor, the reason, or what the doctor said. When asked if he would be surprised to find out JonBenét wet the bed more than he thought, he cut off the question by saying no, regardless of how much she wet the bed, anything short of every night.

JonBenét's bed-wetting most likely had nothing to do with her murder. What is note-worthy is John's detachment from her medical situation and more importantly, John's willingness to put up a front to protect his family. The interactions among the family members, and in this case John specifically with Patsy, help to explain many of the answers they gave in various interviews. Understanding the baseline of the family dynamics contributes to a better comprehension of why many answers seemed bizarre to the outside world, but not to the Ramseys.

John was completely unaware Patsy had panic attacks. Patsy had at least one panic attack prior to the death of JonBenét, and she subsequently had several afterward. John and Patsy never discussed her panic attacks even though they had a tremendous impact on her emotionally. The failure to discuss the panic attacks demonstrated Pasty's lack of comfort with discussing intimate and important aspects of her life with John. Patsy chose not to share with John episodes resulting from extreme stress and anxiety. If Patsy had something to hide involving the night of December 25th, it is highly unlikely she would have ever discussed it with John.

When the interviewers pressed John regarding how he knew Patsy was not involved in the death of JonBenét, he responded, "you live with someone for 18 years, it is pretty hard to keep secrets." As the interviewer pointed out, he had an affair in his first marriage, and like all affairs, they are kept secret, at least at for a while. As with most of John's logic, it does not withstand scrutiny. People keep secrets in marriages all the time. It does not make them murderers, but it certainly discredits his explanation. Furthermore, John and Patsy's relationship demonstrated that each of them kept many intimate and material details from the other.

Since both John and Patsy described their relationship as close, it is not surprising both of them would refer to their interactions on December 26, 1996 as close. They had no feeling of distance between them. In contrast, the police and victim advocates observed considerable distance between the two of them. The victim advocates initially thought the Ramseys were either divorced or separated based on their behavior and lack of interaction. There was a considerable divide between how the Ramseys viewed their interactions on the 26th compared to others who were present. John saw himself as focused on getting JonBenét back while occasionally checking on Patsy. Patsy felt like John was there for her, but taking care of business regarding the expected call and other matters pertaining to the kidnapping. The police and victim's advocates observed a complete void between John and Patsy. Patsy was hysterical and John was not there to comfort her. They stayed in separate rooms and did not interact at all during the morning of the 26th. In the Ramsey's book, they described Detective Arndt as misreading the situation; however, the explanation [John needed to concentrate on the ransom requests, while periodically looking in on Patsy] for John's behavior validated the statements made by the police and victim's advocates. The Ramseys were separate. The physical separation during the morning of the 26th demonstrated that John and Patsy did not gravitate toward each other under extreme stress. They coped with stress independently.

John and Patsy lacked an emotional link. There was no line of communication between them. Neither suspected the other of any wrong-doing. It is probable the Ramseys never discussed the night of

December 25th, 1996, except maybe during the writing of their book. John stated in their book that he and Patsy talked about the murder/investigation constantly. Of course, this is in direct contrast to statements they made during interviews. Patsy stated during her April 1997 interview with the police that it was too difficult to discuss. Both parents believed the other loved his/her children, so murder was out of the question. An accident does not play into the equation because it was seen as a brutal murder, not an accident. The communication within the Ramsey family was no better than the communication between the Ramseys and the police.

Chapter 12 - Legality over Morality

The Ramsey's self-focus and deceptive tactics were clear in January of 1997. The parents said one thing and did another. Most people could not understand why parents would not cooperate with the police, regardless of whether they were suspects or not. And the Ramseys were not cooperating, despite their best public relations' tactics. The Ramseys spent more time trying to justify and explain their cooperation than actually cooperating. As John tried to explain, the Ramseys fully cooperated, but the reason they did not cooperate fully was because they did not trust the police.

The police looked at Jeff Merrick, a former Access Graphics' (John Ramsey's business) employee, within days of JonBenét's murder. John Ramsey identified him as a person of interest regarding the death of his daughter. Mr. Merrick was probably the second, potential suspect in the case after the house-keeper. The police cleared him of suspicion fairly quickly. When he arrived at the police department, he stated, "I'm here, on a murder case, without a lawyer, talking to two detectives, having been pointed out by John Ramsey as a suspect. Now, where is John Ramsey?" (Thomas 2000)

The parent's behavior surrounding the investigation into finding JonBenét's killer(s) generated tremendous publicity and is one of the most troubling aspects of this case. The Ramseys failed to fulfill their moral obligation to their brutally murdered daughter. Within days of the murder of their daughter, the Ramseys transformed from grieving parents into individuals fighting a public relations' battle designed to protect their reputations. The Ramseys focused on protecting themselves, not on finding JonBenét's killer. Even the hiring of their own investigators may have been more about finding exculpatory evidence for them rather than finding the perpetrator. The Ramseys were more concerned about how the public perceived them than fighting for justice for their daughter.

Early in the investigation, the general public was appalled and judgmental toward the Ramseys. Many did not agree with the parents sexualizing their six year-old daughter through beauty pageants. The media presented, and thus the public absorbed, a young girl made to look like an adult. The tawdry beauty pageant pictures showed a little girl stripped of her innocence. This was unacceptable to the public. Even if some in society accepted beauty pageants for young girls, the brutal murder coupled with sexual molestation, exaggerated the outrage they felt toward the pictures and videos of JonBenét performing. The public condemned the Ramseys for allowing JonBenét to enter beauty pageants. The beauty pageants had nothing to do with her murder, but the media sensationalized pageant pictures to the determent of the Ramseys.

The Ramseys behavior surrounding the murder perpetuated the public anger toward them. The Ramsey's initial behavior around the death of their child was purely reactionary, regardless of their involvement. It was not their fault. For example, John Ramsey showed poor judgment in arranging to have his family flown out of the state minutes after he found JonBenét. Obviously, he was not thinking clearly at the time. Not only the public, but the investigators also placed a lot of emphasis on the Ramsey's behavior immediately surrounding the murder of JonBenét. The parents did not react in a manner most people thought grieving, innocent parents should have reacted.

The final element, which caused the public to condemn the Ramseys, was how they dealt with the police. The Ramseys conducted television interviews and hired public relations personnel, all while refusing to fully cooperate with the police. There were many reasons for this approach, but most people chided them for it. The lack of cooperation with the police was one of the most damaging elements and also the one most in the Ramsey's control. The Ramseys chose not to cooperate with the police; and as a result, they remained under the umbrella of suspicion.

Defense attorneys and those untrustworthy of law enforcement would undoubtedly have recommended the Ramseys avoid talking with the police without a lawyer present. This opinion would be true regardless of their guilt or innocence, though it would be even more emphatic if they were guilty. If they were innocent, talking to the police without a lawyer could have resulted in an arrest by an over-zealous police force. There are numerous stories of false convictions and even situations where innocent persons have confessed, though an innocent person confessing is rare. Individuals usually falsely confess when the suspect is mentally impaired, emotionally weak, or the interrogators engaged in some type of unethical coercion. Most persons do not confess to crimes they did not commit under normal circumstances, but it has and will happen.

Early in the investigation, the Ramsey's biggest risk was either a confession or their words being twisted to where the authorities felt compelled to arrest them. From all accounts, however, the Ramseys cooperated with the police on December 26, 1996. Patsy Ramsey called 9-1-1. Both John and Patsy answered police questions on the morning of the 26th without the presence of an attorney. The only hint of non-cooperation was when John told the police Burke did not know anything about what happened. Then, John ushered Burke out of the house. The statements by John were most likely a result of his desire to remove Burke from the stressful situation rather than a failure to cooperate with the police.

Many argue one should never talk to the police without an attorney present because of the risk of arrest. Yet, who would avoid answering questions when his daughter is missing and presumed kidnapped? Even the Ramseys cooperated at this point. It was not until the lawyers were involved did the Ramseys refuse to cooperate. Therefore, it was not the absence of attorneys, but the inclusion of attorneys, which resulted in a lack of cooperation.

In the classic short story *The Lottery*, a small town gathered annually for the stoning of a townsperson, which was supposed to ensure a good harvest. In the first round, the head of each family drew a slip of paper to determine if his family had been selected for the second round. For the family who drew the allotted slip of paper, there was a second round where all family members, regardless of age, drew a slip of paper to see who within the family would be stoned.

In the first draw, Bill Hutchinson drew the slip of paper with the black spot, which means his family had been chosen. Bill's wife Tessie arrived late to the gathering. Once she realized her family has been selected she began to protest the fairness of the circumstances. In a fit of panic and hysteria, Tessie yelled out, "There's Don and Eva. Make them take their chance!" [her son-in-law and daughter, respectively] One of the persons in authority reminded Tessie married daughters are connected to their husbands' family; therefore, Eva is not considered part of her family for purposes of the lottery. In the end, the townspeople stoned Tessie to death.

There are many appalling aspects of this story, as it questions tradition for the sake of tradition, as well as the group/mob mentality. Also, the story highlights the desperate attempts a mother [Tessie] undertook in order to spare her own life. She would forgo one of her child's lives to save her own. The incredibly selfish act further emphasized the shocking set of circumstances surrounding this annual town gathering. Is Patsy Ramsey the modern-day Tessie by putting herself ahead of her child [JonBenét], or is she ultimately allowing herself to be persecuted in order to protect her other child, Burke?

With regard to the investigation, the Ramseys would do anything for their child, other than risk arrest or losing face in public. As John stated in his June 1998 interviews, there is no higher priority than to find JonBenét's killer; however, he would not help the Boulder Police Department because they were out to lynch them. John demonstrated, once again, he would place his own interests ahead of doing what was right for JonBenét. John's actions and even numerous statements contradicted his claims of complete cooperation with the police during the investigation.

Many of John and Patsy's statements may have been technically correct or true, but lacked completeness. As pointed out in Mark McClish's book *I Know You Are Lying*, people do everything to avoid lying. A person will use every aspect of their intellect to justify or find a way to answer a question truthfully, even though the overall answer may be misleading

(McClish 2001). If telling the truth requires the Ramseys to tell the whole truth then they failed miserably throughout the investigation. John appeared more forthright than Patsy, but he has proven when it comes down to it, he will mislead too. When he stated on national television they never hired a public relations ("PR") person (his lawyers hired the public relations person), John demonstrated that perception is more important to him than the truth.

The Ramseys wanted people to believe they were helpless victims of the media, but the Ramsey's chose their actions. The Ramseys accused the media of making false statements and mis-portrayals of them. Claims that probably had considerable validity. However, in *The Death of Innocence*, the Ramseys cited media accounts as to how they knew the police were not conducting the investigation in the best manner. It appears the Ramseys deemed the media unreliable when it was adverse to their cause and reliable when it bolstered their claims or mission.

John Ramsey showed poor judgment throughout the investigation. He failed to accept responsibility for his actions. He even deflected the decision to hire attorneys onto his friend and business associate,

Mike Bynum who advised him to retain counsel. Mr. Bynum is an attorney and acted on the Ramsey's behalf on December 26th and 27th to some extent, until they retained criminal attorneys on December 28, 1996. John blamed his attorneys for his lack of cooperation with law enforcement. At the same time, John touted his extensive cooperation with law enforcement. John's insistence that he and Patsy fully cooperated throughout the investigation significantly impaired his credibility.

Hiding behind lawyers may have been the Ramsey's legal right, but it does not mean it was moral or ethical. Society tries to tie morality to law, but it is simply not the case. Laws are designed to provide order to society, not set a moral compass for society to live by. The Ramsey's response to the murder may have been legally acceptable, but it was morally and ethically corrupt.

On July 18, 1969, Ted Kennedy attended a party on Martha's Vineyard's Chappaquiddick Island. The party was also attended by several women from Robert Kennedy's presidential campaign the preceding year, including Mary Jo Kopechne. Though there were many holes and inconsistencies in the timeline and story, sometime after 11:00 p.m.

Ted Kennedy left the party to drive Ms. Kopechne to her hotel. A troubling contradiction, Ms. Kopechne told no one of her departure and she left her purse and hotel key at the party. After leaving the party, Ted Kennedy drove off Dike's Bridge and into Poucha Pond with Ms. Kopechne in the car.

According to later analysis, Ms. Kopechne may have lived for over two hours while breathing through an air pocket in the upside down submerged car. She died from a lack of oxygen, not drowning. Ted Kennedy left the scene and walked back to the party. On the walk, he passed four houses where he could have called for help for Ms. Kopechne. Ted Kennedy did not call the authorities from the cottage where the party took place. He also did not call at any time during the entire night after he returned to his hotel room. The individuals he spoke to at the party did not contact the authorities because Ted Kennedy told them he was going to contact the police. He did not notify the police until he realized her body had already been discovered.

Ted Kennedy allowed a woman to die in order to save his reputation. Though he could never be charged with a more serious crime, he remained under an umbrella of suspicion. In some ways, the Ramsey's position in the murder investigation of

JonBenét was similar to Ted Kennedy's decision. By Kennedy avoiding the police in the early part of the investigation, it probably saved him from going to jail, but resulted in a dark cloud cast over him for the rest of his life.

As the Ramseys admitted in their book, *The Death of Innocence*, their lawyers' primary goal was to keep them out of prison. Since the Ramseys placed their desires and judgments behind those of their lawyers, the Ramseys, by default, also placed staying out of prison as a higher priority than finding JonBenét's killer(s). As a result, the Ramseys avoided prison, but they have a blanket of suspicion and guilt smothering them indefinitely.

Chapter 13 - "Cooperation is a two-way street!"

John Ramsey was likely not involved in the murder or cover-up of JonBenét's murder, even though his behavior was suspect, and he deceived many throughout the investigation. The authorities cleared John's hand-writing as author of the ransom note. He did not have a motive. No one obtained information indicating any sexual inappropriateness on his part at any time. However, suspicion still hangs over him.

The Ramsey's legal team treated the Ramseys as defendants in a criminal trial rather than possible suspects in a murder investigation. As a result, the Ramseys viewed their circumstances through the same lens. The lawyers prepared for an indictment against their clients. The Ramsey's legal team focused on keeping their clients out of jail, not on finding the killer(s) of JonBenét. Unfortunately, the Ramseys approached the investigation in much the same way.

There is no presumption of innocence in an investigation. It is not a criminal trial. Investigators need to be open-minded; however, suspects or potential suspects need to be eliminated or charged.

Investigators must eliminate suspects based on information collected. Investigators must look in all directions and utilize tactics that may never be admissible in court. When a suspect or potential suspect exhibits signs of deception or unwillingness to cooperate, it causes investigators to engage and pursue them. The Ramseys were incapable of understanding an investigator's perspective or job.

John Ramsey regularly mentioned the presumption of innocence, though the Ramseys were not in the middle of a criminal trial. They were tried in the court of public opinion, but the presumption of innocence does not apply there either. In a criminal investigation, the investigators approach everyone with an open but alert mindset. Investigators pay attention to discrepancies in statements, conviction behind responses, and outright deception, among numerous other indicators from the interviewees. The Ramseys failed miserably in this arena. The Ramseys exhibited numerous and chronic indicators of deception. For investigators, deception is usually equated with guilt, even though they are not always the same.

Regardless of the Ramsey's exhaustive attempts to show their cooperation with the authorities, the Ramseys failed to cooperate throughout the investigation. They tried every avenue, except actual cooperation. Though the reasons and circumstances changed, their lack of cooperation was fairly apparent throughout. Even the Ramsey's comment, "Cooperation is a two way street" is an acknowledgement by them they were not cooperating. Though at this point, their justification was the authorities were not cooperating with them, an interesting perspective when working with the police.

During the June 1998 interviews, John Ramsey stated he remembered seeing a truck behind the Barnhill's house when he looked out Burke's window on the morning of December 26, 1996. From all accounts, this is the first time John mentioned this to the police. This could be a vital piece of information to the investigation and John chose to hold this information for 18 months.

During her June 1998 interviews, interviewers asked Patsy if she noticed anything unusual when she got home on the night of December 25, 1996. She responded, "If I had, by God you would have known it before today…" Patsy proclaimed she would have notified the police if she noticed something out of place. Yet, Patsy, mainly following John's lead, failed to cooperate throughout the investigation. Why would this factor have changed her desire to cooperate? She implied she would have been forthright with information pointing toward an intruder. Throughout the investigation, Patsy's illogical actions and behaviors mitigate the authenticity of her theoretical cooperative gesture.

During a March of 2000 interview on the *Today Show*, Katie Couric asked John and Patsy Ramsey if they would agree to an interview on the spot. Both responded, "Absolutely." When Ms. Couric brought up their refusal to go to the police station on December 27th, John responded they could not leave the house because of all the cameras and reporters. Once Ms. Couric highlighted the obvious weakness and hypocrisy of John's argument, he went on to explain Patsy was physically incapable of leaving the house. However, John could have gone to the police station. There was nothing preventing him from going. Friends and family cared for Patsy, as John maintained his distance; therefore, he did not need to stay for Patsy's sake.

As of December 27th, the Ramsey's had not assembled their criminal defense team. John made the decision not to allow the police to interview Patsy and him at that time. Most probably, John was not thinking clearly. Also, consistent with his baseline personality, John thought he deserved different treatment than others. Even his gut reaction to flee the city 20 minutes after finding his daughter dead demonstrated his initial reaction was toward himself, not his child. John's desire to protect his ego would not allow him to admit as much on national television. John created several reasons why they did not go with the police to be interviewed. Ultimately, the Boulder Police made a crucial error by not insisting the Ramseys conduct interviews when they were leaving their home on December 26th.

If any one of the numerous persons the Ramseys identified as suspects responded to the police in the same manner as the Ramseys, they may still be under the umbrella of suspicion as well. John and Patsy would have been appalled if another potential suspect in this case hid behind lawyers and refused to be interviewed, all while going on national television to discuss the case. None of the other potential suspects appreciated the implication of involvement in a child's murder; however, they did not overtly convey feelings of shock at the looming police questioning. The Ramseys positioned themselves above the investigation. The stress of the situation exaggerated John Ramsey's feelings of self-importance and arrogance. John and Patsy never flinched when providing names of potential suspects to the police, but they showed utter distain at the mere thought of their involvement in this heinous crime.

On *20/20* in March of 2000, Barbara Walters asked John and Patsy Ramsey how they felt when they were prime suspects in the murder of JonBenét. John expressed the outrage they felt upon realizing the police considered them suspects. Interestingly, when a technicality favors him, John chooses to ignore it. The police never identified the Ramseys as prime or official suspects. The police treated them as suspects and the public believed it to be so, but the official position of the police remained that the Ramseys were "under an umbrella of suspicion." A young child was found viciously murdered in her house while her parents were home and there were no signs of forced entry. The parents refused to cooperate. It is not clear why John failed to understand why they were targeted by the police.

The Ramseys believed resisting the police and refusing to provide information would eliminate them from suspicion. Common sense escaped the Ramseys throughout the investigation. The onus is, and always has been, on the Ramseys to cooperate and ensure they are cleared from suspicion. The authorities have no obligation to cooperate with suspects' requests. The police have an obligation to thoroughly investigate a crime. John and Patsy's approach came across as arrogant, which has done nothing to ingratiate them with the police or public.

While on television, the Ramseys regularly agreed to be interviewed by the police. They would agree to cooperate with the police on national television, only to rescind the offer in private. The Ramsey's PR tactics were selfish and uncaring with respect to their daughter.

> I promise you; whatever scum did this, not one man on this force will rest one minute until he's behind bars. Now, let's grab a bite to eat.
>
> – Sergeant Frank Drebin, Detective Lieutenant Police Squad, *The Naked Gun*

John Ramsey's statements on national television paralleled the above quote, without the intended comedic value. Unfortunately, the Ramsey's compassionate statements about cooperation were not supposed to be a joke. Most of what was conveyed by the Ramseys on television provided nothing but entertainment. The questions and statements were completely empty. John Ramsey told Lou Smit during his June 1998 interviews he was 100% committed to cooperating with the investigation. When asked if there were any limitations on this commitment, John responded, "None. As long as we are dealing with an objective investigation."

The subject of a polygraph examination ("lie detector test") recurred throughout the investigation. During his April 1997 interview, the police asked John Ramsey if he would take a polygraph examination. John reluctantly agreed to allow a polygraph examination. There was miscommunication, or more accurately, disagreement and fighting between the Boulder Police and the District Attorney's Office regarding this point. No one administered a polygraph on John. This situation became the source of debate and ongoing questions as to whether John was ever asked to take a polygraph examination or not, and did he agree or refuse.

John believed his response was affirmative to the question of taking a polygraph examination, which is probably an accurate evaluation of the interview segment. The police failed to administer the examination at that time or subsequently; therefore, they believed the offer was disingenuous. As with most elements of the investigation, both sides contested the other's recollection of the events.

During numerous television interviews, John Ramsey was asked if he would take a polygraph examination. Further irritating the police, John's responses hedged and contained various caveats. Based on his regular pattern of agreeing to things on national television, only to recant them in private, the police believed his willingness to take a polygraph examination was not legitimate.

During his interview on the *Today Show*, John indicated that it never crossed his mind to volunteer to a polygraph exam because he was not interested in proving his innocence. To the contrary, almost all of John's media and propaganda efforts were designed to prove and demonstrate his innocence. The Ramseys were obsessed with the public's perception of them, yet they never took the necessary steps to assist in demonstrating their innocence.

John refused to take a polygraph examination from the FBI because he claimed they lacked objectivity. John believed the FBI had advised the Boulder Police to look closely at the family. It is hard to blame him for not wanting to take a polygraph examination from an organization that may well believe he was culpable. However, John's refusal demonstrated his lack of cooperation throughout the investigation. Suspects, or even witnesses, do not normally get to pick who interviews or interrogates them.

Based on the FBI indicating it would need a week lead time in order to administer the polygraph, John Ramsey described the FBI as having "other motives in mind." John did not understand the preparation necessary prior to conducting a polygraph examination, but he inferred preparation by the FBI must have indicated it had ulterior motives. In addition, a polygraph examination is a form of interrogation; it is not just a means of determining truthfulness. Since the FBI polygraph examiner would interrogate John and Patsy Ramsey that is likely the real reason they refused. A Ramsey described "objective" polygrapher would merely ask the questions and read the machine and individual.

If one believes the Ramseys are innocent then many of the decisions made by the Ramsey legal team were deplorable. There are a lot of *ifs* in that statement though. Not only did many of their decisions leave the element of guilt looming over the Ramseys, more importantly, it prevented the investigators from pursuing other leads more aggressively. What did the Ramseys have to lose by taking an FBI polygraph? If one or both of them failed, they would be right where they were at the time, still under the umbrella of suspicion. In addition, polygraphs are not admissible in court. If the Ramseys passed the FBI polygraph examination, it would have been monumental. It would have provided them with heightened credibility within the investigation. Sure, there would still be naysayers within the Boulder Police Department, but it would have allowed the investigation to move forward.

On *20/20* with Barbara Walters, in March of 2000, both John and Patsy Ramsey responded they would take a lie-detector test. Patsy followed her affirmative response pointing out lie detector tests are not admissible in court. She also referred to it as a "kind of voodoo science." Most likely, Patsy's statement was made after she had already taken and failed several privately-administered polygraph examinations.

In May of 2000, Larry King had former Boulder Police Detective Steve Thomas on the show with John and Patsy Ramsey. The interactions and discussions between the participants were heated. During the program, the topic of taking polygraph examinations was broached. Mr. Thomas stated that even with the Ramsey hired and paid for polygrapher, it took Patsy three times to pass the polygraph. Though John Ramsey was quite confrontational throughout the program he did not correct or deny Mr. Thomas' statement. As many in the Boulder Police Department suspected, Patsy would not be able to pass a polygraph examination; and hence, the core reasoning behind why the Ramseys refused an FBI polygraph. It may have resulted in the police zeroing in on Patsy even more.

One of the themes John and Patsy have repeated is parents could not brutally kill their own child. During Patsy's interview on *Burden of Proof* in April of 2000, she stated, "What was done to JonBenét could not have been done by a parent." Unfortunately, parents have committed violent acts of this nature. Thankfully, it is rare. It is horrific to think parents could do such things to their children, but they have. The Ramsey's logic here is flawed and does not provide deflection of blame away from them.

John made the *logic-based* argument, "A person doesn't go throughout their lives as a normal human being. One night turn into a monster. Slaughter their daughter. Go to bed and get up and act normal from there on. That doesn't happen…" Who was John implying acted normal after the murder of JonBenét? He additionally stated, "In these kinds of cases, virtually all of 'em I suspect, where there is child abuse in a family there's a long history. And that's not the case in our family." John started out his statement as if he was an authority or has the statistics behind all child murders, but then he finished by saying, "I suspect," which indicated he was merely speculating. When statistics pointed away from the family, John touted the findings; however, when the data pointed toward the immediate family, John exclaimed the police needed to look beyond them. John's inability to prove his innocence resulted in many desperate statements woefully below his normal intellect.

During the *Today Show* in March of 2000, this exchange took place:

> Ms. Couric: In your book, you--you've written what you call a chronicle of cooperation. But let me give you, to challenge that, a chronicle of uncooperation [sic]. In January, you'll answer questions but only from the officers your attorney chooses, and only at your attorney's office, and Patsy can only be interviewed for one hour. Police then cancel an interview in April, because the FBI concludes that the conditions they've agreed on with you would make it unproductive. In other words, ground rules. These things don't seem to add up to a great deal of cooperation with the authorities.
>
> Mr. Ramsey: Well, you've got to understand what our predicament was. We realized within a week that we were the only targets in the investigation. And any good attorney will tell the police, 'Look, if you're trying to get my client, go ahead and prove it, but you're not going to talk to my client.' The police concluded on December 26th that it

must have been the parents, because it's always the parents, and that became their conclusion. They solved the crime, and then they just tried--tried to prove it. So it was a very difficult predicament for us.

There is no cooperation here. John explained exactly why they did not cooperate. John's response laid out the reasons behind why they did not cooperate, rather than illustrating their ongoing cooperation.

Though the relationship between the Ramseys and the police was contentious, interestingly, with regard to some things, the Ramseys did cooperate. They provided records and allowed searches. The detectives interviewed other Ramsey family members. Granted, there were usually some limitations on the cooperation, but there was a level of cooperation. On the contrary, when it came to interviewing John and Patsy Ramsey the cooperation ceased.

The Ramsey legal team most likely had very specific reasons why they fought so hard to control the interview process. The Ramsey's legal team hired former FBI profiler, John Douglas, to evaluate the Ramseys because some on the team questioned the innocence of the Ramseys. Mr. Douglas' assessment of innocence reduced many of the team's concerns, though it most likely did not alleviate them.

Though the Ramsey's attorneys were there to defend their clients not render judgment, their actions revealed their hand. Clearly, the Ramsey attorneys believed there was a huge risk in allowing the police to interview Patsy. They requested to allow Patsy to answer her questions in writing. The attorneys requested Patsy and John be interviewed together. The attorneys may have had reason to believe Patsy's statements could incriminate her or lead the police to think she was involved in the death of JonBenét. An emotional, unscripted Patsy was an unpredictable client. Though it cannot be known what the legal team actually believed about her innocence, the team was at least very concerned about her susceptibility to an admission or an incriminating, flippant utterance. The legal team exerted tremendous effort to protect Patsy from the investigators.

Fearful the District Attorney's Office would utilize a grand jury to compel the Ramseys to testify, John Ramsey sent a letter indicating full cooperation to the Boulder District Attorney in April of 1998. Consistent with many statements made by the Ramseys while on their many PR tours, John offered to cooperate but only under his strict parameters; they could only be interviewed by the Boulder District Attorney's Office, not the police. Certainly, the letter John sent demonstrated some level of cooperation by the Ramseys, but it was out of self-interest and fear of a grand jury that compelled him to make this gesture.

At times, John was totally consumed by what happened to him rather than the fact JonBenét was murdered. It is almost as if the injustice he experienced was his primary focus. During his June, 1998 interviews he stated: "My family, children have been affected…Plus, JonBenét lost her life."

Chapter 14 - Politician in Training

John Ramsey is a highly intelligent and successful businessman. John's ability to read and interact with people suited him well in the business arena. His successes left him with an air of cockiness, which remained below the surface, unless provoked. John's personality and his desire to maintain his ego contributed significantly toward how he dealt with the authorities throughout the investigation.

Within hours of discovering the ransom note, John Ramsey conveyed two things very clearly: he was not involved in the murder/cover-up and he will deceive if he deemed it necessary. John's statements and actions early in the aftermath of JonBenét's murder demonstrated he was not privy to what went on in the house on the night of December 25[th,] though many of his behaviors were bizarre and hard to explain.

When asked about the condition of the house on December 26th, John told three different police officers the house was secure the previous night (Thomas 2000). As with many of John's statements from that morning, he later changed his story about the security of the Ramsey house. Notwithstanding, John's original statements to the police indicated he was not building a case for an intruder. John presented the information as he saw it. If John was involved in anyway, he would have tried to lead the police toward concluding an intruder entered the house. He would have identified unlocked doors and windows. He would have mentioned to the police the numerous individuals who had keys to the house or missing house keys. Instead, John told the police few persons outside the immediate family had house keys. John actually built a case against an intruder during the early hours of the investigation.

The second, and most compelling evidence John was not involved in JonBenét's murder, was his immediate response to his daughter's murder. Upon placing his daughter's dead body on the floor of the house, John stated, "This had to be an inside job." This was John's initial, visceral response to finding JonBenét murdered in the basement. If he were involved, he would have been much more concerned about getting caught, thus he would have immediately pointed blame away from himself and others close to him. John's utterance showed his true feelings and emotions. Based on the circumstances he observed, JonBenét was killed by someone very close to them. Not the statement of a murderer or conspirator who wanted to divert blame. As a side note, the Ramseys completely left out that

John uttered this statement in their book, *The Death of Innocence*. Though not written from the objective perspective, the absence of one of the most critical statements in the case demonstrated John's shift in focus.

The need to deceive and protect also coated many of his statements and actions throughout the investigation. Since John was not involved, why the deception? As will be shown, John Ramsey misled and confused the investigators in order to: protect Burke, stay out of prison, and a complex assortment of anger and ego. John's demeanor and deceptive posturing placed him in the cross-hairs of law enforcement and the general public. John spent considerable time and energy perpetrating deception, though it was not to conceal his guilt. There were many instances where John misled, deceived, and ran loose with the facts. Here are some of his misleading statements:

#1) Statement regarding Burke on December 26, 1996 – On the morning of December 26, 1996, John Ramsey decided Burke should leave the house. He would send him to a location where adults could look after him, but it would also keep him out of the stress of the situation at their house. As John and Fleet White took Burke out of the house, Officer

French attempted to delay Burke from leaving. Officer French told John he needed to question Burke about the events of the previous night. John responded that Burke did not know anything, and he slept through the night. And with that, Burke left the Ramsey residence. There is no detailed information on what questions Officer French asked Burke, answers provided, or further interaction among them.

Prior to John's statement to Officer French, there is no indication John even spoke to Burke about what he heard or may have seen the previous night. John stated he told Burke JonBenét was missing, and Burke began to cry. Furthermore, even if John had briefly spoken to Burke about the previous night, it would have been cursory. The gravity of the situation would have certainly required a deeper probe. Any nine year-old child is prone to lie, withhold information, or exaggerate. With his sister potentially taken from a room down the hall, Burke would have been in the best position to have witnessed something.

John's dismissive comment to Officer French conveyed an air of deception. John decided removing Burke from the crime scene was more important than allowing the police to gather critical information. The extent of John's intentions is unknown; however, he demonstrated early in the investigation he would make potentially deceptive statements to protect those around him.

#2) Hiring PR firm - The hiring of a public relations executive was one of the first measures taken. In early January, 1997, lawyers hired by the Ramseys, hired a public relations executive, Pat Korten. According to Pat Korten, he met with John Ramsey right after he was hired in January of 1997. This directly contradicts John's statements and later portrayals through various media outlets. On *Larry King Live* in March of 2000, the following exchange took place:

> Mr. Ramsey: Let me clarify one other...
>
> Ms. Ramsey: We didn't have PR people.
>
> Mr. Ramsey: We didn't have a PR firm...
>
> Mr. King: You never did?...
>
> Ms. Ramsey: No. That was a myth.
>
> Mr. Ramsey: That's -- our attorneys hired a media information person. They were getting 300 phone calls a day into their office. They couldn't cope with it. They hired someone that could be a focal point for all these calls

from the media. That got translated by the
media as a public relations spin doctor.

John tried to use a technicality to twist the story in
his favor. The Ramseys did have a public relations
person and John met him. John was aware they had
a public relations firm working for them. Once the
hiring of a PR firm turned against them, John wanted
to distance himself from it. He did so by trying to
change the public's perception of his PR team,
though it did not change the truth of the matter.
Validating the inaccuracy of his above statement,
during John's interviews in June of 1998, he
specifically stated hiring media consultants was the
biggest mistake they ever made, which is an
interesting statement, based on the many
questionable actions by the Ramseys.

John's misleading statements on the *Larry King Live*
television show presented him in a more favorable
light. John tried to confuse and obfuscate the facts
around their hiring of a PR representative in an
attempt to regain his reputation. John believed he
had been wronged by the media and made many
attempts to right that wrong, even if it meant
manipulating the truth.

#3) Setting conditions for interviews - On *Larry
King Live* in March of 2000, John Ramsey claimed

they did not set conditions for the interviews. Larry King identified how conditions were set involving the request to only be interviewed together, with their lawyers present, and in their doctor's office. John responded that no conditions were set. At first, he alluded to the fact it was his attorneys who set the conditions, but he did not even admit to that. He emphasized how defense attorneys should protect their clients from over-zealous police departments. John positioned himself on both sides of the question by denying conditions were set, but at the same time he defended why conditions needed to be set. It is hard to understand how John thought his response was accurate. Of course conditions were set. Since the Ramseys hired attorneys, communications went through lawyers, but the Ramsey's attorneys, who were acting as their agents, presented interview conditions.

#4) Providing a list of suspects - During his interview on *Larry King Live* in March of 2000, John Ramsey indicated he never gave the police a list of suspects from the neighborhood. John may be technically correct that he never provided a paper list of suspects from his neighborhood, but he certainly provided the police with a detailed list of individuals he suspected of wrong-doing in the death of his daughter.

John Ramsey spent considerable time during his two official interviews identifying potential suspects in the murder of JonBenét. During his April 1997 interviews, John stated he thought it was odd Fleet White did not scream after he found JonBenét's body. In actuality, Fleet screamed for help as he ran up the basement stairs after John discovered JonBenét's body. John regularly casted blame on those around him based on their unusual behaviors, but the Ramseys exhibited odd behaviors throughout the ordeal and he discounted those due to the stress of the situation. He did not apply the same logic and consideration to others.

The White's became the target of John's suspicions. When asked about the ransom note, he stated Fleet White used his name [John] a lot. He also indicated Priscilla White may be the writer of the ransom note. John went further and stated Fleet White had duct tape similar to the tape found over JonBenét's mouth. In the Ramsey's book, *The Death of Innocence*, John stated, "Maybe the police told Fleet and Priscilla that we had turned on them and named them as suspects; but that simply wasn't true." (Ramsey 2001)

John Ramsey may not have specifically called Fleet and Priscilla White "suspects," but he made every indication he believed they should be. He let the police know of every unusual behavior they exhibited. Both John and Patsy directed police attention toward the Whites whenever they could. The Whites were in the cross-hairs of the Ramseys, yet John denied it in their book.

John Ramsey, during his April 1997 interviews, described Linda Hoffman-Pugh's behavior as "very bizarre." Linda asked Patsy Ramsey for money just prior to the murder of JonBenét, and she complained to Patsy about a fight with her sister. During his June 1998 interviews, John identified a man from church, JonBenét's photographer, and his secretary's boyfriend as suspicious persons. In some way, each of the persons identified by John Ramsey exhibited unusual behavior, though as with the Ramsey's behavior, it is not clear if it had anything to do with involvement in JonBenét's death or not.

Bill McReynolds is one of the many people John Ramsey identified as a potential suspect. John indicated Bill McReynolds could have gotten JonBenét into the basement because she trusted him. JonBenét would have also trusted Patsy, Burke, himself, and many other family members. John did not point this out. During the same interview, John stated "people" were telling him early on

McReynolds was the one who did it [killed JonBenét]. John cleverly utilized unnamed third parties as his source for identifying Bill McReynolds as a possible suspect for the police to consider. He provided minimal articulable facts or substantiation, but nonetheless John conveyed his suspicions of Bill McReynolds.

#5) Lack of official investigative information - In later television interviews, John Ramsey expressed concern over his lack of official knowledge about the investigation. He claimed to only have been informed about the investigation by the television and through rumors; however, during his April 1997 interviews with the authorities, John indicated he reviewed police reports prior to the interviews. He responded he "scanned them." His daughter was murdered, and the police interviewed him as a potential suspect in her murder, though his answer implied he did not review the police reports thoroughly.

John clearly reviewed the police reports extensively as he later identified what he considered errors within the reports. John couched his answers in a manner most favorable to him and his family, not in an attempt to portray a true representation of the facts. Scanning the police reports versus thoroughly analyzing them conveyed an air of innocence. John postured himself in a manner that construed he was there to tell the truth, not regurgitate answers prepared by his attorneys. A comprehensive review of the police reports could imply John needed extensive preparation in order to answer police questions; therefore, John wanted to present a natural, unprepared demeanor. Even still, John could not resist the urge to point out inconsistencies in the report that made him look untruthful or guilty, though that very action contradicted his statement regarding his preparation for the interviews.

#6) Burke during the 9-1-1 call – John Ramsey stated on several occasions his son Burke slept through the 9-1-1 call on the morning of December 26, 1996. The following exchange took place on the airing of the *Today Show* in March of 2000 and is an example of his apparent denial:

> Ms. Ramsey: Give me one reason. What have we ever done in our past that would give anyone reason to believe we'd kill our daughter?

> Ms. Couric: And yet some things just don't make sense. There are no clear signs of forced entry, leading police to suspect the killer was no stranger. They also think the

ransom note is bogus. Who would take the time to write a three-page note at the scene of the crime and risk being caught? And then there's the question of the 911 call. You called 911 at 5:52. Burke was asleep. And yet the tape of the 911, as you all know, was enhanced in a lab and revealed a conversation in the background, apparently, between you, John, and your son Burke.

Mr. Ramsey: OK...

Ms. Couric: How you do explain this?

Mr. Ramsey: The facts are that Patsy and I told the police that Burke, to our knowledge, was asleep and had been asleep until I got him up to go to Fleet White's house later that morning.

John response exhibited a classic trait of deception, though it is not clear to what extent. John stated the "facts are," but he did not actually identify what happened the morning of December 26, 1996. He did not answer the question. All John attested to was what he and Patsy told the police. This is a traditional subconscious technique to avoid having to tell an overt mistruth. He did not deny Burke's presence during the call. He also did not say what happened. John only described what he told the police. Regardless of what actually happened during the morning, John's above statement is accurate because he is only acknowledging what was previously stated.

When it comes to deception by the parents pertaining to Burke, it is reasonable to believe they were protecting him. There could be more ominous reasons why they protected him, but at a minimum they tried to ensure Burke was kept out of the investigation for his mental well-being. If John or Patsy acknowledged Burke's presence during the 9-1-1 call, it would additionally impair their integrity, and it would bring Burke into the investigative fold. As a result, both parents have strong motivations to continue to perpetuate their previous story, regardless of the implications on the investigation.

#7) Bonus - During the April 1997 interviews, John Ramsey stated he did not know the amount of his 1996 bonus ($118,223) until he went back and looked at it. In the same interview, he later stated his bonus appeared on every one of his pay stubs for the remainder of the year. John inferred that anyone who saw one of his paychecks would have seen the bonus amount. However, John claimed to be unaware of his own bonus amount. For John to not know his bonus, he would have had to ignore his pay stubs from February through December of 1996.

Companies do not pay bonuses in a vacuum. Bonuses are usually tied to meeting various goals or metrics. John would have had discussions with his supervisor regarding the bonus prior to the payment. Other executives around John would have also likely received bonuses at the same time. There would have been meetings pertaining to bonuses for executives. Regardless, John was in a position of knowledge; and therefore, he would have had numerous opportunities to view documentation for his bonus within his official position, much less on a personal level – reviewing his paychecks.

According to Patsy's statements during her April 1997 interviews, she indicated John mentioned the similarity between the ransom note and his bonus on the morning of December 26th. John was immediately aware of the closeness of the ransom request amount and his recent bonus. Based on Patsy's statement, John intentionally deceived the police when he said he was unaware of his bonus amount. John deliberately downplayed his knowledge of the $118,000 amount because he thought it would make him, or someone close to him, look guilty.

Though John was not directly or even indirectly involved in the murder and cover-up of JonBenét, his actions and statements drew immediate criticism and alarm. John acted with an air of aristocracy and entitlement while identifying friends and acquaintances as culprits of the brutal murder of his daughter. He also refused to acknowledge the lack of cooperation he exhibited throughout the investigation. John avoided accountability for any of his actions. He stated it was Fleet White's idea to go on national television on January 1, 1997. John further attributed the hiring of public relations persons to his lawyers. He also deflected much of his failure to comply with police requests onto his lawyers. John's inability to accept responsibility for his actions generated a negative public image and an aura of distrust with law enforcement.

In March of 2000, Katie Couric interviewed the Ramseys on the *Today Show*. When asked why he went to the basement on the morning of December 26th, John responded that he wanted to check on the window below the grate in the basement. He told Ms. Couric it was open and broken. John's answer implied the presence of an intruder. In previous interviews, John had already acknowledged he was the one who broke the window, and the window was sometimes open to let out heat.

During John's June 1998 interviews, he was asked about the book *Mindhunter*, by John Douglas.

Mindhunter details how to conduct staging around a crime. The police found the book in John and Patsy's bedroom during one of the searches. John claimed he never read the book, and he did not know it was in the house. It is plausible John was not aware of the presence of the book; however, his response should be viewed skeptically.

In later interviews, John Ramsey devoted most of his effort toward building the case for an intruder. In order to demonstrate his innocence and that of Patsy, he felt it was necessary to convince people an intruder was present.

John Ramsey's behavior during the investigation materially impacted progress toward solving JonBenét's death. Though John was most likely uninvolved and unaware of what happened on the night of December 25th, 1996, his failure to cooperate and antagonistic attitude resulted in additional investigative resources being focused on him. Many of John's decisions have limited investigators' ability to determine exactly what happened that night. However, there is probably a part of John that realizes he does not really want to know who was involved in JonBenét's demise.

Chapter 15 – "There is a Killer on the Loose!"

I didn't -- I couldn't read the whole thing I -- I had just gotten up. We were on our -- it was the day after Christmas, and we were going to go visiting, and it was quite early in the morning, and I had got dressed and was on my way to the kitchen to make some coffee, and we have a back staircase from the bedroom areas, and I always come down that staircase, and I am usually the first one down. And the note was lying across the -- three pages -- across the run of one of the stair treads, and it was kind of dimly lit.

It was just very early in the morning, and I started to read it, and it was addressed to John. It said 'Mr. Ramsey,' And it said, 'we have your daughter.' And I -- you know, it just was -- it just wasn't registering, and I -- I may have gotten through another sentence. I can't – 'we have your daughter.' and I don't know if I got any further than that. And I immediately ran back upstairs and pushed open her door, and she was not in her bed, and I screamed for John.

-    Patsy Ramsey, *CNN*, January 1, 1997

Prior to a formal interview with the Boulder Police Department, John and Patsy Ramsey went on *CNN* to tell their story. It is not clear how their television appearance helped the investigation or even the point of doing it. Were Patsy's comments sincere or were they contrived? Patsy's introduction to the general public was a combination of a rambling diatribe mixed with extreme emotion. There are many explanations for Patsy's bizarre behavior, such as her being overly medicated, confused, stressed, or just traumatized by the whole experience.

During her June 1998 interviews, Patsy told the interviewers she was diagnosed with post-traumatic stress disorder ("PTSD"). According to the National Institute of Mental Health, post-traumatic stress disorder is an anxiety disorder developed after a person experiences a dangerous or life-threatening situation. The person's fight-or-flight response to danger has been impaired. The person reacts with stress or fear even though he is no longer in a dangerous situation.

The symptoms associated with PTSD include: flashbacks to the triggering event, bad dreams, feeling emotionally numb, depression or guilt, easily frightened or startled, and memory loss. PTSD is diagnosed by a psychiatrist, doctor, or psychologist who has experience with mental illness by talking with a person who is experiencing some or all of the symptoms previously noted. For a person to be diagnosed with PTSD, the National Institute of Mental Health states the person must have all of the following symptoms for at least one month: at least three avoidance symptoms, at least one re-experiencing symptom, at least two hyper-arousal symptoms, and difficulty functioning in daily life.

With PTSD, a doctor cannot run a blood test to identify it or take an x-ray to see it. A diagnosis of PTSD is almost completely based on input from the person being diagnosed and observation by the doctor. The diagnosis has a significant subjective nature to it, and there is no consistent, reliable manner for verifying a diagnosis. As a result, someone could fake having the disorder, and there is no test to validate the assessment. However, it is highly unlikely Patsy Ramsey faked the symptoms in order to be diagnosed with PTSD. It would be quite reasonable for her to have had PTSD. She experienced a tremendous tragedy and many of her behaviors after the murder were consistent with the symptoms of PTSD, though symptoms vary significantly from person to person. Furthermore, Patsy never tried to use PTSD as an excuse for her answers during any interviews or as a defense against what she may or may not done on the night of December 25, 1996.

Whether Patsy did or did not have PTSD has no bearing on her involvement in the murder/cover-up of JonBenét. Regardless of her role, the circumstances under either scenario would be more than enough to result in significant mental trauma. The events of December 25th and 26th severely impacted Patsy's state of mind and mental health. It was an event she never got over. She passed away in 2006 after a battle with cancer.

It is quite reasonable to assume Patsy did have PTSD. The implications of which are monumental. It is possible she could have no or minimal recollection of the events on the night of December 25th. Patsy could have potentially denied involvement conscious-free without having a firm understanding of what exactly happened or what she did. However, this is unlikely. Patsy's behavior seemed to indicate she was well aware of what transpired on December 25th and 26th.

A diagnosis of PTSD could lessen the validity of Patsy's statements. Confusing and contradictory statements may be explained due to the trauma of the events. Statements that seemed to implicate her in the crimes may hold less value if her mental condition was impaired. Since the evaluation of symptoms and the severity of the disorder are subjective, the introduction of PTSD to the equation only serves as a factor when assessing Patsy's behavior and statements.

Patsy's mental condition played a material role in all of her statements and actions. She most likely used it as a crutch to explain or justify inappropriate or conflicting statements. Though Patsy was very unstable and she was understandably distraught, she seemed to only feign ignorance or confusion when it suited her. Undoubtedly, the Ramsey legal team went to great lengths to limit Patsy's interaction with investigators. The legal team's positioning was likely due to Patsy's mental condition, coupled with their concern over her involvement in the events that transpired during the night of December 25th, 1996.

Patsy's behavior surrounding JonBenét's death was odd, volatile, and suspicious. It does not directly mean she did anything criminal, but it certainly warranted additional investigation. The Ramsey's stonewalling with the Boulder Police Department did not alleviate concerns or suspicions regarding her. Patsy conveyed a multi-faceted facade with an air of cunny, which made it hard to disregard her as a possible conspirator.

During the Ramsey's first television interview on January 1, 1997, Patsy Ramsey shuddered as she stated, "There is a killer on the loose!" Regardless of who killed JonBenét, this was a true statement, even if it were her. People do not like to lie. Even if on a subconscious level, people struggle to find ways to tell the truth, though it may be a partial truth.

Patsy deceived throughout the investigation for a number of reasons. The most pressing reasons were to protect Burke and deny involvement in any part of the murder/cover-up of JonBenét. Patsy had some level of culpability in the crimes, which needed to be concealed. Patsy also went along with John in many of his statements regarding cooperation, but she was not the driver of those comments or the lack of cooperation overall. Patsy was too distraught to have been an active decision-maker during the investigation.

#1) Preparation for interviews - During her official June 1998 interviews, investigators asked Patsy what she did to prepare for the interviews. Patsy responded that she prayed. She also indicated she met with her attorney, and she "thinks" he gave her a document from her previous interview. She thumbed through the document provided to her. The Ramseys spent a tremendous amount of money on lawyers, investigators, and various criminal experts. The team dedicated hours strategizing and planning. The Ramsey legal team placed significant focus on obtaining information and evidence. The legal team even requested the actual questions prior to the scheduled interviews. Within the context of an army of Ramsey lawyers and investigators, Patsy responded as if none of this was occurring. The lawyers had an obligation to advise the Ramseys. Of course, the lawyers gave Patsy advice on how to answer questions, especially since most believed Patsy was the target of the police's interviews. The lawyers devised a strategy and provided Patsy with all the information they acquired.

Patsy's casual response to the question regarding preparation downplayed the significance of her attorneys' advice and counsel. Maybe she believed it violated her attorney/client privilege, but her answer was misleading. Patsy tailored answers to ensure she looked her best and most innocent, no matter what actually transpired. The justification behind Patsy's misleading and evasive answers was complex. It was a combination of self-protection due to involvement, the perceived injustice thrust upon her, and her determination that much of the requested information was irrelevant to the death of JonBenét. Regardless, the pattern of deception was present.

#2) John Ramsey's first marriage affair – The Boulder Police asked Patsy about the extent of her knowledge of John's affair during his first marriage. To their surprise, Patsy claimed to be completely unaware of his affair. Patsy's sisters and mother were aware of the affair. It is not clear how Patsy was not aware of the affair when the Boulder Police thought it was common knowledge among the Ramsey family and friends. No one acted in a manner that would indicate a secretive nature to the information regarding the affair. Patsy's denial was not expected by the police.

It is highly unlikely Patsy did not know about John's earlier affair. She may not have cared. It may not have been of any consequence to her. However, Patsy probably believed the police thought it was significant, and they planned to use it against John somehow. As a result, Patsy felt inclined to deny her knowledge of the affair in order to protect John from additional unwarranted persecution. It had no bearing on the murder investigation, but it is another example of Patsy answering questions in a less-than-forthright manner.

#3) "Sunday afternoon thing" - During her April 1997 interviews, Patsy referred to JonBenét participating in pageants as a "Sunday afternoon thing." In contrast, Patsy, Nedra (Patsy's mother), and others spent considerable time preparing JonBenét for her pageant contests. Patsy hired dance instructors. Custom designed outfits were made for JonBenét at tremendous cost to the Ramseys. During family Christmas letters, Patsy boasted of

JonBenét's accomplishments on the pageant circuit. Though there were many facets to JonBenét as a person, to Patsy, the pageants were a large part of the time she spent with her daughter.

Patsy deliberately downplayed the pageants. Patsy wanted to counter the media hype surrounding the pageants. Patsy resented the media casting JonBenét as a sex symbol or as somehow different (in a negative manner) because she participated in the pageants. Patsy wanted to protect the image of her daughter and let people know she was a regular kid who happened to participate in pageants.

#4) JonBenét's underwear - At one point, Patsy indicated she had never seen the underwear JonBenét was wearing when she died. The underwear in question did not fit JonBenét. It was too big for her. At first, it seemed odd for a child who seemingly placed a high value on appearance, to be wearing baggy underwear. The detectives later determined Patsy purchased the underwear during a trip to New York City shortly before Christmas, 1996. Patsy originally purchased the underwear for her niece, who was much older than JonBenét. JonBenét begged her mother to allow her to keep them, and Patsy relented. Patsy repeated this story on several occasions. It was a well-known story to her family and friends.

Patsy most likely deliberately deceived the police when she stated she did not recognize the underwear. On the vanity front, she did not want people to think she would let her beautiful, graceful daughter wear poorly-fitted, baggy underwear. This would be implausible to most people, but for a woman obsessed with how things looked and what people thought, it is a reasonable possibility. The other reason for deceiving would be driven by a more sinister motive. At some level, Patsy tried to mislead the police with regard to what happened to JonBenét. Patsy may have believed her comment could have generated confusion for the investigators and possibly led them to believe an intruder was involved; hence, investigative focus would have been diverted away from the Ramseys.

#5) Practice ransom note – During her official interviews, the police never directly asked Patsy Ramsey whether or not she wrote the "practice" ransom note. Patsy also never volunteered any information regarding her involvement or lack of involvement in the writing of the practice note. Patsy's failure to come forward and admit she wrote the note can be viewed as a denial.

The practice ransom note was found on the same pad of paper as was used to write the actual ransom note. It is generally believed the practice note was written just before the ransom note and by the same person who wrote the ransom note. Most believe the practice note was an initial, failed attempt to start a ransom note. The practice ransom note contained the following: "Mr. and Mrs. l" with the last line believed to be the start of the "R" in "Ramsey." Extensive testing determined the same pen was used to write the practice note as the ransom note, and the hand-writing was considered similar.

Pam Griffin, who was involved in beauty pageants in Boulder, Colorado, said Patsy Ramsey told her she wrote the practice ransom note for an innocent purpose (Thomas 2000). The police were unable to confirm this statement. Though Ms. Griffin's allegations are unsubstantiated, Patsy could have written the note weeks before the death of JonBenét for any number of innocent reasons. This is the most plausible explanation because if Patsy had written the note in conjunction with the cover-up of her daughter's death, she would not have casually mentioned it to Ms. Griffin.

Under this scenario, the writing of the alleged practice ransom note had no connection to the murder and cover-up, other than the similarities in the hand-writing between the two notes. Patsy may have believed her writing the practice note was immaterial to the investigation; therefore, she did not feel inclined to divulge the information to the police. Furthermore, both Patsy and John believed the police were out to get them. As a result, she probably believed if she either changed her story or tried to explain the practice ransom note, it would only implicate her in some way. To Patsy, she withheld information not because of her involvement, even though she was involved in the cover-up of the murder, but because she had to keep the police from persecuting her. Patsy used her discretion, and she determined the police did not need to know the truth about the practice ransom note.

#6) Knowledge of the ransom note - Based on Patsy's statements as of the April 1997 interviews, she had not fully read the ransom note. During the interviews, Patsy stated she could not bear to read the entire note when she found it, but she did not elaborate on whether or not she read the note between December 26th and the April 1997 interviews. She responded to questions as if she was completely unaware of the contents of the ransom

236

note. At one point during the April 1997 interviews, Patsy said she did not know what the interviewer meant by a "small foreign faction."

During Patsy's June 1998 interviews, she stated she read the entire ransom note several times. Notwithstanding, her responses to questions regarding the ransom note implied an ongoing unfamiliarity with the note's content. During the interview, Patsy's responses to questions involving the ransom note were quite similar to earlier responses when she claimed to have only read part of the ransom note. Patsy could not distinguish between what she was supposed to know about the note on December 26, 1996 compared to what she knew or should have known as of her June 1998 interviews. Patsy's internal confusion regarding her knowledge of the ransom note at different junctures reflected in her disorganized and illogical responses to ransom note-related questions.

In Patsy's interview on *20/20* in March of 2000, she stated, "I believe it said 'listen carefully.' "Something like, 'We have your daughter.'…" At this point, Patsy acknowledged she has read the ransom note numerous times; however, she still feigned as if she was completely unfamiliar with the ransom note. Why was she incapable of speaking intelligently about the ransom note? She had already claimed her reasoning for using "and hence" was due to the number of times she had read the note and written its contents. Patsy's relationship with the ransom note was never straight-forward or consistent.

Many of Patsy's statements and answers to interview questions were filled with inconsistencies. Patsy presented an inconsistent storyline, and her conviction constantly changed. She regularly altered her recollection of events with the simple explanation that she was confused. One example occurred during Patsy's June 1998 official interviews, she stated, "I know there was a red heart on her hand or forehead." The strength of her statement contrasted sharply with most of her other responses. Patsy answered most questions with "I think" or "maybe." Her response to the red heart on her hand/forehead was emphatic. The following day, after speaking with her lawyer, Patsy said she could not distinguish between whether she saw the heart or read about it. She could not remember if she saw it, because she recently read the autopsy report and she had an image in her head. It is not clear what the implications are regarding Patsy's changed statement. It is quite troubling if she was not able to distinguish between seeing something on her dead child's hand versus something she read in a report. Based on this retraction alone, Patsy's statements lack credibility.

Patsy's statements during her official interviews in June of 1998 regarding what she wore on Christmas were troubling and nonsensical. Though it is very difficult to understand what she was trying to say, most of what can be cobbled together implied that Priscilla White had the same jacket as Patsy. Patsy appeared to be trying to tie the jacket to Priscilla rather than herself. Patsy tried to say that she wore Priscilla's jacket, but only if she had gotten cold. However, her story made no sense and there was no reason why she would have been wearing Priscilla's jacket and not her own, especially since all indications were that she wore her own jacket on Christmas. It appeared to be another attempt by Patsy to implicate one of the White's in wrong-doing. The implication is predicated on Patsy's belief that the police could tie the jacket to the death of JonBenét.

Patsy hinted during her June 1998 interviews that she believed Fleet knew the ransom note a little too well. She said he worked in, "…oil kind of business, so he [Fleet White] said…" implying she could only attest to what he told her. Patsy also referred to Fleet White's eyes as "wild" during the same interview. Numerous, objective persons made similar comments about the Ramseys in and around the death of JonBenét, and these statements were dismissed as foolish by the Ramseys. It could be argued Patsy was merely telling the authorities all she could in an effort to help find the killer(s) of JonBenét. On the other hand, Patsy was indirectly tying Fleet's mannerisms to the death of JonBenét. Her motives appeared disingenuous.

Another example of Patsy's "helpfulness" occurred when interviewers showed Patsy a number of pictures of various items from the Ramsey house. The pictures were taken around the time of JonBenét's murder. The purpose of the picture display was for Patsy to identify anything out of place or unusual. One picture was of a scarf. Initially, Patsy said the scarf looked strange. It did not belong. However, once interviewers told Patsy the picture was taken on Christmas morning and it was from John's roll of film, she backed away from her comment.

Understandably, during the morning of December 26th Patsy was completely distraught. She described herself as "out of her mind!" Buried in the grief of the situation, Patsy could not initially assist the police understand the circumstances of her daughter's disappearance. Yet, over the years there were many times she was emphatic with her statements, as if there was no question to what she stated. If any of Patsy's statements were later found to be incorrect, she claimed stress or confusion. She cannot have it both ways. Investigators were unable to take her emphatic statements as fully correct, and ignore the several occasions where her statements were proven wrong. There was no way to know which instances she remembered correctly and when stress or deception impaired her response.

Except for statements made on December 26th, 1996 and times when evidence pointed to the contrary, John and Patsy have, more or less, stuck to their official statements. There are inconsistencies between the two stories, but each has maintained their respective timeline. If Patsy had significantly changed her version of events, it would have been viewed negatively by the police and could have resulted in her arrest. Therefore, Patsy had to stay with her story; otherwise, she would have further eroded her credibility with the authorities.

Chapter 16 – Not under the Umbrella

Burke Ramsey was a month shy of his tenth birthday when his sister, JonBenét, died. He was one of only four known persons in the Ramsey house on the night of December 25, 1996. Investigators provided minimal resources toward understanding what Burke knew or did on the night in question. Due to his age, the police treated him delicately. If Burke were a few years older at the time of JonBenét's murder, he would have been viewed *very* differently. He would have likely been under suspicion. His age was a major obstacle to any potential implication of wrong-doing. Under Colorado law, a child under the age of 10 could not be tried for a crime, even in juvenile court.

In the Ramsey's 1995 Christmas Letter, Patsy stated Burke was the tallest kid on his basketball team. Though Burke was very young when JonBenét was murdered, he was not small for his age. There were no other indications he was physically, mentally, or emotionally advanced beyond his years. He was quiet and did not exhibit exceptional maturity.

In 1994, Burke hit JonBenét on the cheek with a golf club. Patsy took JonBenét to a plastic surgeon. The doctor did not believe surgery was necessary or needed (Maloney 1999). There is minimal information about this occurrence. Incidents of this nature happen all the time with children, but in light of a brutal murder, all previous accidents need to be re-evaluated. During Patsy's April 1997 interviews, she indicated Burke also hit JonBenét in the leg at one point, but she did not provide details on when or the severity. Probably to the benefit of Burke's mental health, there is minimal information on his behavior and statements. Even information Burke provided as part of the investigation has been kept fairly confidential.

Burke's young age at the time of the incident made it difficult to interpret or understand his answers and corresponding behaviors, though many were strange. Like his parents, he was peculiar, and he did not act in a manner consistent with what would have been expected. There was a limited behavioral baseline for Burke; therefore, it is difficult to determine whether exhibited behaviors were out of character for him or simply abnormal when compared to other children who experienced similar tragedies.

Dr. Suzanne Bernhard conducted Burke Ramsey's initial interview on January 8, 1997 at the Child Advocacy Center in Niwot, Colorado. He was also interviewed over three days in June, 1998, and he testified before the grand jury. Burke told Dr. Bernhard he felt safe. Dr. Bernhard found this comment unusual as many people in Boulder were scared, but Burke, whose sister was murdered in their home, felt safe. Dr. Bernhard indicated Burke's statement was inconsistent with her experience. A child who has a family member killed usually does not feel safe.

In light of the fact JonBenét was killed in her house while her parents were home, it is understandable many children were frightened. Children need to feel safe and secure. The brutal murder of a classmate caused many children to re-think the security their parents, teachers, friends, and community provided them. In contrast, Burke did not show fear. There are many potential explanations. Burke may have still been in denial about what happened or unable to grasp the gravity of the situation. He may have believed his parents were more conscious about security; therefore, it could not happen again. Many things could have been running through his head to justify his feeling of safeness. There is also the possibility he was not being honest. He was terrified, but he wanted to come across as strong, though this would not be consistent with his overall demeanor

According to observers of the interview, Burke showed little warmth toward his family, but was protective of them. Dr. Bernhard noticed Burke had a hard time talking about his family, and she believed it could indicate he felt there were things he should not say. This is not a statement of fact, but it was her professional interpretation of his reactions. Burke's reactions could have been a result of his natural personality, but the responses were still noteworthy to the doctor.

According to Dr. Bernhard, Burke displayed a tremendous lack of emotion. She explained it could have been a result of shock or how he coped with the tragedy, but it also could have been due to a lack of attachment to his family. Burke accepted the murder of his sister, but he was void of the normal emotion expected from a child in this situation. For example, Burke told the doctor he was "getting on with his life." Also, when Burke drew a picture of his family he did not include JonBenét, which is something most children avoiding doing for years after the death of a family member because of the realization of the loss is too much to bear. According to Dr. Bernhard, the drawing of his parents indicated his father was distanced from Burke and his mom lacked power.

During Burke's interview, Dr. Bernhard asked if he knew what happened to his sister. After the question was asked, he showed signs of irritation for the first time during the interview. Burke responded, "I know what happened, she was killed." He additionally explained someone took her quietly to the basement, and took out a knife or hit her on the head. There is no indication either parent had spoken to Burke about what happened to JonBenét prior to this interview.

During Patsy's April 1997 interviews with the police, she stated she had not discussed anything about JonBenét's death with Burke, as it was too difficult for her. Burke said the only question he asked his dad about JonBenét was where the body was found. Burke's answer indicated he knew more than he divulged. Regarding JonBenét, Burke only asked his dad, "Where did you find the body?" Of all the questions to ask, this was an unusual inquiry. Why did he not ask what happened to her? Or, who killed her? One theory speculates he was involved or witnessed what happened to JonBenét, but he was not involved in the aftermath; as a result, he did not know where her body ended up. It is pure conjecture as to what Burke may or may not have been hiding, but his answers have troubling implications.

During Burke's interview with Dr. Bernhard, he showed anxiety when asked about "uncomfortable touching." Burke placed a board game on his head during this line of questioning. There is no information on how much the doctor pushed Burke with these questions. Since the autopsy has led many experts to believe someone molested JonBenét prior to the night of her death, Burke's input on this topic is crucial to understanding whether something inappropriate was going on in the house prior to the night of December 25th, 1996. Though prior molestation may not have been connected to her death, it is a consideration. Burke's responses leave the possibility of molestation within the family open, but do not provide any clarity on it.

One component of Burke's answers differed from what his parents had stated. According to accounts of Burke's official interview, after returning home from the White's party on the night of December 25, 1996, JonBenét walked up the spiral stairs to bed just ahead of Patsy. Burke's comments directly contradicted his parents' account of events during this timeframe. John and Patsy both stated on numerous occasions JonBenét was asleep when they got home, and John carried her to bed. Burke's account of the night's events was consistent with what John told police on December 26th, though he later denied those statements. Based on the varying accounts, the sequence of events upon the family's arrival home is in question. Someone's account is wrong.

John and Patsy had no obvious reason to lie about JonBenét being asleep when they arrived home on the night of December 25th. Whether JonBenét was asleep or awake could have easily been explained away, similar to the pineapple situation. However, by John and Patsy telling the authorities JonBenét was asleep when they got home it set a clearer timeline for when an intruder could have entered the house. It also reduced the possibility investigators would think Burke and JonBenét roamed the house after they got home.

If JonBenét was awake when the family arrived home on the night of December 25th, it does not implicate the parents in any wrong-doing, other than lying to the police. If either parent changed his/her story it could be detrimental to their already questionable credibility. As with most elements of their recollection of events, the Ramseys could have pled ignorance and probably have survived the fall-out.

It is also possible Burke did not remember correctly, but it is less likely since Burke's memory error was consistent with what John told several police officers on December 26th. Furthermore, Burke identified where JonBenét was in the order walking up the spiral stairs. This small detail adds credibility to his statement.

Burke indicated he stayed in bed on December 26, 1996 till around 7:00 a.m. when his father woke him. Burke stated he was awake when his mom made the phone call [9-1-1]. Burke further claimed he did not speak to his parents prior to his father waking him to go to the White's house. Both John and Patsy's statements were consistent with Burke's comments. This is refuted by the technical voice analysis indicating Burke's voice can be heard on the 9-1-1 call. The Ramsey's defense team has attempted to discredit the technical analysis conclusions.

According to John Ramsey, when he woke Burke on the morning of December 26th, he told him JonBenét was missing and Burke cried. This is contradicted by Fleet White who claimed Burke never asked why police were in the house or where JonBenét was. Nor did Burke ever ask why the family was not going on vacation (Gentile 2003). There is no information on Fleet White's proximity to the entire discussion between John and Burke. If Fleet's account is accurate, it does not necessarily prove anything other than another example of John

Ramsey's failure to be completely forthright in his statements and more unusual behavior by Burke.

Dr. Bernhard was concerned Burke denied he had an ongoing bedwetting problem. She indicated most children are honest about things of this nature during an interview. Burke's response demonstrated he was not fully forthright during the interview. Also, when asked if he had any secrets, Burke responded, "probably, if I did, I wouldn't tell you, because then it wouldn't be a secret." (Unknown 1999 (Bonita Papers)) Though there appears to be times during Burke's January 1997 interview where he was not completely truthful, it is hard to imagine he would have known what to lie about. For example, he did not remember eating anything on the night of December 25th. If he had pineapple with JonBenét during the night, he would have had to know not to disclose that, unless he was just overly evasive with his answers.

During Patsy's April 1997 interviews, she stated she had not talked to Burke about what happened to JonBenét. During the June 1998 interviews, Patsy told the investigators she did not discuss with Burke anything about his three days of interviews with the police, though she did not elaborate on whether they had ever discussed JonBenét's death. Burke indicated the interviews were fine and boring. When interviewers asked Patsy if Burke could have hurt

JonBenét, she responded, "It wouldn't have been Burke." Why Patsy would say it "wouldn't" have been Burke versus it "couldn't" have been Burke or it "wasn't" Burke? Does she have knowledge of what happened that led her to say, "it wouldn't have been Burke"? When asked how she knew Burke did not hurt JonBenét, she said it was because she had talked to Burke about JonBenét. Patsy gave no additional explanation. Either she had spoken to him about JonBenét or she had not. Patsy's responses indicate a lack of complete forthrightness regarding Burke.

In Mark McClish's book, *I Know You Are Lying*, he states guilty persons rarely directly deny they committed the act. A guilty person will usually respond in a manner that sounds like a denial but is not, such as "I wouldn't do that." By a person saying he "wouldn't" do something the person is saying he would not normally do that as opposed to actually delivering a denial (McClish 2001). Patsy's use of the contraction "wouldn't" fits the book example almost exactly. Patsy is saying it would be out of character for Burke to have hurt or killed his sister, which is undoubtedly a true statement, but not a denial.

There is minimal information from the interviews of Burke Ramsey. Compared to other persons involved in this case, little has been written about Burke. It is not clear or well documented what he was asked or how he responded. Burke's only direct contradiction

251

to his parent's statement was that JonBenét was awake when the family arrived home on the night of December 25, 1996. On the morning of December 26, if Burke did go downstairs to talk to his parents, it would be somewhat surprising since he never mentioned it in his interview with the authorities. A nine or ten year-old talking to an authoritative figure would most likely not be aware of the consequences of discussing various aspects of his whereabouts during the morning of December 26, 1996. Then again, many of Burke's reported responses were inconsistent with what most expected.

Excluding the specifics of this case and Burke Ramsey in particular, the likelihood a nine, almost 10 year old, would engage in molestation and sexual games involving torture, is low, but well within the parameters of documented violence and sexual inappropriateness by children. Though it is possible and it has happened, even with children significantly younger than Burke, it is hard to believe it could happen.

John and Patsy did not coordinate their stories surrounding the murder of JonBenét and aftermath. The lawyers may have paid attention to the various statements and ensured they were consistent, but the Ramseys did not actively coordinate their statements.

Their relationship was not close enough for them to discuss in detail their thoughts, feelings, and actions surrounding the murder of JonBenét. If there was an exception to this, it would have been with regard to Burke. At some point, the parents likely decided for Burke's well-being, they needed to totally keep him out of this. The agreement may never have actually been explicit between the parents, but there was an effort to protect Burke from the investigation.

There is limited information on the behavioral characteristics of Burke since JonBenét's murder. Regardless, if he exhibited questionable behavior it would prove nothing. It would certainly raise the suspicion toward him, but it would not prove or necessarily indicate anything regarding his activities on the night of December 25, 1996. It is unusual he has not had any run-ins with the law. If he did, it would be attributed to mental trauma he endured from having his sister murdered and being accused of it in the media. Therefore, absent a confession, there is no evidence pointing directly toward Burke Ramsey as one of the perpetrators of JonBenét's murder or cover-up.

Chapter 17 - Pathways

Surrounding the JonBenét Ramsey murder, we are more certain of some elements while others remain a mystery to this day. We know that the manner in which the police handled the crime scene and investigation, coupled with the questionable actions of the District Attorney's Office, significantly impaired any chance of definitively determining what happened to JonBenét. There are strong indications John and Patsy Ramsey deceived throughout the investigation, which further erodes the likelihood the full truth about the events of December 25, 1996 will be known.

John Ramsey deceived the investigators and the public because of his ego, anger toward the police, to protect Burke, and his belief any change in his story would result in his arrest. John was less than completely forthright regarding the following items or events:

- Claimed he never hired a PR person
- Stated he cooperated with the police throughout the investigation
- Burke's presence during the 9-1-1 call [call analysis is debatable]

- On December 26th, telling Officer French Burke slept through the night, when John was not in a position to make that statement.
- JonBenét was asleep when they came home on the night of December 25th [Contradicted by his own and Burke's statements]
- Statements around the broken window and glass found
- Awareness of his February, 1996 bonus

Patsy Ramsey deceived, either intentionally or due to stress/memory loss regarding the following items or events:

- Regarding writing the ransom note and practice note
- Her location when she yelled for John on the morning of December 26th
- Burke's presence during the 9-1-1 call [call analysis is debatable]
- Significance and time committed to beauty pageants
- Knowledge of the underwear JonBenét wore when she was killed
- Her knowledge of John Ramsey's affair during his first marriage

- JonBenét being asleep when they came home on the night of December 25th [Contradicted by John's and Burke's statements]

There were many small indications of an intruder, though the main piece of evidence pointing toward an unknown individual(s) present in the Ramsey home is the unaccounted for touch DNA located on and near JonBenét. The DNA analysis does not tell us when it was placed there or how it got there, only of its presence. Based on the lack of unaccounted for fingerprints, any potential intruders most likely wore gloves, which significantly reduces the likelihood the "touch" DNA will tie to one or more intruders. The crime scene was contaminated. Placing the bulk of the case on forensic evidence would be irresponsible and unproductive. The DNA evidence is significant because of what it could mean, but it is likely irrelevant to the murder and subsequent cover-up. There is the possibility a stranger was present during the night of December 25th, but it is not the most likely scenario, even in light of the DNA evidence.

Most intruder theorists utilize the concept of an intruder as being mutually exclusive to Ramsey involvement. That is not necessarily the case, and possibly, an intruder may have been there at the request or knowledge of one of the Ramseys. Based on the preceding analysis, if there was an intruder he would have been there to see Patsy. There is almost no conceivable theory taking into account the circumstances of this crime where one or more unknown intruders entered the Ramsey house on December 25th, 1996. As a result, it leaves only intruders known to one or more of the Ramseys. If Patsy wrote the ransom note then it would have been someone she knew very well. She knew the person well enough to cover-up the fact he killed her daughter.

If there were one or more intruders, who were they? Most likely, any intruder was someone very close to Patsy Ramsey. *It could have been a lover, though there is no evidence she ever had an affair.* If this was the case, how come no one even knew of or mentioned him to the investigators? How did he get in? Why was he there? Under this scenario, we move from analyzing the evidence to almost pure conjecture and speculation. This theory is predicated on the assumption there was an intruder(s) and Patsy wrote the ransom note to cover for someone she loved, excluding those with whom she lived. However, most of the evidence pointing toward an intruder is tenuous and certainly debatable.

Murder portion

In evaluating the act of killing JonBenét, there was little information excluding a given suspect or theory. There was also minimal information or evidence pointing definitively toward a given suspect or theory. When looking at the murder portion of the events, the potential perpetrators are divided into six categories with some of the categories only containing one option. The possible perpetrators of JonBenét's murder include:

- Patsy Ramsey
- John Ramsey
- Burke Ramsey
- Family, friend, or close acquaintance
- Stranger
- Unknown

The elements of the actual murder include:

- Rope
- Garrote
- Baseball bat (possible)
- Flashlight (possible)
- Skull fracture
- Strangulation

Of the physical items listed, only the rope cannot be definitely tied to the Ramsey house. Of the three items listed from the Ramsey house, an intruder could have reasonably found and utilized the baseball bat and/or the flashlight to produce the skull fracture. It is unlikely an intruder would have found the paint brush handle and broken it to use as part of a strangulation device. Based on the weapons utilized to kill JonBenét, they do not point conclusively toward someone from inside or outside the house. The only exception to this is the garrote, which would point toward someone from inside the house based on its secluded location just outside the wine cellar in the basement.

The two injuries that resulted in JonBenét's death were the strangulation and skull fracture. Almost any able-bodied person could deliver these types of injuries to a six year-old girl. Some are more likely than others, but in general the cause of death does not include or exclude anyone. No one from the above list can be excluded based on the circumstances of the murder.

Just as Patsy's or John's DNA on JonBenét would not prove one of them killed her, the discovery of evidence pointing toward an unknown person's presence at the crime scene does not prove an intruder killed her either. The presence of unknown DNA on JonBenét could indicate foul play by an unknown intruder though it is most likely due to events not tied to her death.

As a result, when analyzing the actual murderous act, there is no clear answer as to who committed it. Since most of the items used in the murder of JonBenét came from inside the house, it is more likely the killer came from inside the house or was intimately familiar with the house. When weighting the likelihood of someone from inside the house committing the murder versus someone intimately familiar with the family and house, it leans toward a person from inside the house. It would be more logical for someone coming from outside the house to bring the necessary weapons to molest and/or kill their intended target. The actual murder does not point toward or away from anyone definitively.

Cover-up portion

After JonBenét died, without question, measures were taken to confuse and conceal what actually happened to her and why it transpired. The ransom note was not intended to obtain money for the return of JonBenét. Many components of the ransom note were designed to obfuscate the identity of the perpetrators ("small foreign faction"). Someone most likely wiped JonBenét's genital area in an attempt to conceal any sexual molestation. Her underwear and pajama bottoms may have also been pulled back up to further conceal the appearance of molestation. Someone placed duct tape over her mouth, which was likely placed there either after she was unconscious or dead.

The above listed actions and items demonstrate a cover-up was conducted after the murder of JonBenét. Why would someone try to cover-up a murder with a perceived kidnapping? And who would benefit from a cover-up? As with the actual murder, we will assess the possible suspects and associated means/items utilized to complete the cover-up. One of the following possible suspects concocted the cover-up:

- Patsy Ramsey
- John Ramsey
- Burke Ramsey
- Family, friend, or close acquaintance
- Stranger
- Unknown

The elements of the cover-up include:

261

- Ransom note
- Pad of paper and pen used to write the ransom note
- Duct tape
- Wiping of the body
- White blanket & pajamas (not clear if part of cover-up or not)

The ransom note was written on a pad of paper from within the Ramsey house with a pen also from within the house. Since both of the items used in the crafting of the ransom note came from within the Ramsey house, it points strongly toward the persons inside the house. It is unlikely an intruder would use items from within the house as they would have to know for certain the items would be present and accessible. Further, the pen was placed back in the container where it was stored, a subconscious act done by someone concerned about the placement of the pen.

As stated in previous chapters, only under a few highly improbable pathways can the ransom note be authentic. In those scenarios, the ransom note would point toward someone outside of the immediate family. Under the vast majority of the scenarios, the ransom note was written to deflect blame. A scenario where blame is being deflected would directly benefit the Ramsey immediate family members (John, Patsy, and Burke) as a ransom request points away from the family.

It is inconceivable Burke Ramsey, at the age of nine, would have had the intellect and presence of mind to scheme and implement a cover-up involving a detailed ransom note. There were no similarities between Burke's handwriting and the ransom note. Burke is not a viable perpetrator for writing the ransom note and carrying out the other components of the cover-up.

John Ramsey had the intellect to carry out the cover-up and the potential motivation based on the deflection of blame benefiting him. However, the police quickly cleared John as a potential author of the ransom note, even though the Ramsey's refuting of hand-writing analysis negates this conclusion. On the morning of December 26, 1996, John's actions demonstrated a lack of involvement in the murder and/or cover-up. For example, John's initial comment after finding JonBenét's dead body was, "This had to be an inside job." This is certainly not the comment of a person who went to great lengths to conceal a murder by crafting a supposed botched kidnapping. Furthermore, all of John's comments to police during the morning pointed away from an intruder possibility; the opposite tact he would have taken if he was in the process of perpetrating a cover-up. If John were involved in the cover-up, he would have cast suspicion toward one or more intruders during the morning of December 26th. John Ramsey did not construct and implement the cover-up.

Patsy Ramsey's hand-writing has never been cleared as a match against the ransom note. There are considerable similarities between Patsy's writings and the ransom note. Numerous experts have identified Patsy Ramsey as the author of the ransom note. Patsy's statements regarding the ransom note have been inconsistent and incriminating.

Red and black fibers from the jacket Patsy wore the night of December 25th – morning of December 26th matched fibers pulled from the duct tape placed over JonBenét's mouth. The duct tape has never been proven to have come from the Ramsey house. John and Patsy have both denied having similar duct tape in the house. When John Ramsey found his daughter's body, he immediately ripped the duct tape off of her mouth and threw it on the wine cellar floor. The duct tape never left the wine cellar, until it was taken into police custody. And Patsy never entered the wine cellar on December 26th. It is plausible the fibers were on the wine cellar floor and could have attached when the tape was thrown on the floor, but the overall implication is Patsy most likely handled the duct tape while wearing the jacket.

Patsy yelled for John upon finding the ransom note. Patsy had not even checked JonBenét's bedroom prior to yelling for John. Patsy already knew JonBenét was gone. Patsy may have entered or looked into JonBenét's room prior to finding the note, but all of her statements, excluding on the morning of December 26th, indicate she did not. Therefore, either Patsy deceived the authorities regarding not having looked into her daughter's room prior to finding the note, or Patsy knew JonBenét was missing without so much as checking her bedroom.

The evidence points strongly toward Patsy Ramsey as the person who orchestrated or was involved in the overall cover-up. If Patsy conducted the cover-up, for whom was she covering?

As stated above, the actual murder does not point definitively toward any one person or grouping of persons. Therefore, we have to back into who killed JonBenét from the cover-up, through a process of elimination. Someone strangled JonBenét to death during a sexual game that went too far. Her death was an accident. The blunt trauma to her skull was possibly an impulsive reaction to the realization she was dead. There is no clear evidence as to how this blow was completed or with what item. It remains an unknown.

We have four possible options for who could have accidently killed JonBenét, and who Patsy Ramsey would feel compelled to protect. John Ramsey, Patsy Ramsey (herself), unknown person intimately connected to Patsy Ramsey, and Burke Ramsey. Most of John's actions and statements indicated he was not involved in the murder or cover-up. Though Patsy could have certainly felt compelled to protect John, it is unlikely she would have chosen to protect him over one of her children. The couple, though distant and unattached, remained steadfast in their belief the other was not guilty. Both John and Patsy stated if they knew the other was involved they would have turned them in. Though their statements are questionable at best, it is reasonable to believe at some weak moment one of them would have turned on the other. There was no evidence of any sexual abuse by John against JonBenét. More importantly, there was also no evidence John sexually abused any of his other children, and one would expect to see a pattern.

John's behavior during the investigation into JonBenét's murder indicated he would put his interests before his daughter's interests. John showed a selfish and arrogant side that demonstrated under the right circumstances he would not do the right thing. However, even though John may have been potentially capable of a horrific act, his actions and statements on December 26, 1996 override any predilection toward self-preservation. John was not involved in the murder or cover-up of JonBenét.

Patsy had no motive to kill her daughter. Patsy was consumed with her physical condition relating to her cancer, which ultimately killed her. There is no evidence Patsy ever sexually abused JonBenét or anyone else. It is also hard to imagine a scenario where Patsy would have struck JonBenét in the skull hard enough to produce the resulting fracture. Even in a complete fit of rage, Patsy's behavior would lead one to believe her natural response would be to breakdown emotionally, not respond in rage. Patsy loved her children.

Patsy would, however, have motivation to protect herself if she did kill JonBenét. Patsy is a viable perpetrator in the death of JonBenét, but it is extremely difficult to envision a scenario where she would have been able to strike her daughter. Further, if Patsy did accidently kill JonBenét she would have been present at the moment her daughter died. Though self-preservation may have been a secondary thought, Patsy would have likely believed medical treatment could save JonBenét. She would have called for help. This cannot be said for sure, but Patsy would have most probably done everything she could to save her baby, regardless of the implications on her personally.

Since the blunt trauma happened after the strangulation, the indication is that the person's immediate response to the perceived accidental death of JonBenét was rage and anger, not compassion. All indications are that Patsy responded to almost everything with compassion and sympathy. Patsy would not have struck her daughter in the head in response to her apparent death, even if she believed it was her fault. She would have cradled and held her. To the contrary, if someone summoned Patsy to a scene where JonBenét was lying dead, her response would have been different. She would not be able to save JonBenét because she had been dead for quite some time. There was no chance to revive or save her.

Though most likely in complete shock and near collapse, Patsy had to focus on the problem at hand: someone she loved dearly would have to explain a sexual game and accidental death that occurred in the middle of the night. To protect a person she loved, she had to devise a plan to alter what happened to deflect the blame away from who accidently caused JonBenét's death. If Patsy covered for someone else, and it was not John or herself, limited other scenarios remain.

The third possibility is Patsy covered up an accidental death for someone she was very close to, but is not known to investigators in this case. This is a low probability scenario as it is unlikely someone who had an extremely close relationship with Patsy would not have been identified during the investigation. It is not clear if investigators ever received all of the Ramsey's phone records, receipts, etc. This would have helped identify any potential close persons. It is also certainly plausible the investigators missed a key individual in this case due to sheer incompetence. However, there is a very narrow window of possibilities where this option could have taken place.

Individuals who fall into this category include:

- Lover
- Other family member (known, but not suspected)
- Someone Patsy attributed with saving her life from cancer
- Someone who Patsy brought into JonBenét's life and feels guilty for this

The introduction of any one of these individuals would indicate there was at least a fifth person in the Ramsey house on the night of December 25, 1996. There is no evidence Patsy had a lover or any unidentified close friend/companion. This above list merely identifies potential individuals Patsy would be willing to protect

If Patsy had an unknown lover or very close friend, he would have entered the Ramsey house without notice by anyone other than Patsy and JonBenét. Undoubtedly, this would not have been the first time this happened. The person entered the house on several other occasions with questionable intentions. The scenario becomes harder to create and explain the more one ponders such circumstances. This is a plausible, but unlikely scenario.

The possibility of an extended family member's presence on the night of December 25th, 1996 would be reasonable, since it was Christmas night. Though, it would require it to be a relative who could be away from home without the need of an alibi. No one readily fits the criteria. It is not a likely scenario.

The final possible scenario that could have resulted in the accidental death of JonBenét involves her brother Burke. Burke was only nine years old at the time of his sister's murder. He was too young to be tried and convicted for a crime. Initially, he was thought to be too young to be capable of causing the death of JonBenét. Burke was a tall, skinny, quiet kid. He was ushered out of the house on the morning of December 26, 1996 before the police could thoroughly interview him.

There is *no* clear or compelling evidence Burke had anything to do with the death of JonBenét. The only two things keeping Burke in the bucket of possible perpetrators are his proximity (in the house) and the presumption Patsy completed the cover-up. It would explain the subsequent bizarre behavior of Patsy. John's anger, rather than his knowledge or involvement, drove his behavior. Unfortunately, it is the most plausible scenario. And it is regrettable that this is the most likely scenario. It would be much easier and more comfortable to identify a convicted child molester or some other dredge in society.

Though this scenario is the most plausible, it is merely a theory.

Using Patsy's actions and behaviors to back into what happened has a potentially significant flaw. It does not point directly toward who is responsible for JonBenét's death. It is a conclusion by default. It is possible that there is a more plausible explanation that has yet to be identified. As with many aspects of this case, the unknown continues to haunt us.

If Patsy lost one of her children, she would do whatever was necessary to protect her only remaining child. Maybe it was an accident. Maybe Patsy never knew exactly what happened, but someone woke her up and told her something was wrong with JonBenét. Patsy may have never asked the individual exactly what happened. It is likely John was completely unaware of what happened. And to this day, he may only have some fleeting thoughts about the roles Patsy and Burke played in JonBenét's death.

Chapter 18: "I didn't kill my baby"

It is likely one individual known well to JonBenét entered her room between 11:00 p.m. and midnight on the night of December 25, 1996. The perpetrator woke JonBenét from a deep sleep. This is not the first or even second time this has happened. Periodically, this individual has woken her in the middle of the night to play some sort of game. JonBenét was not fearful of this individual, but she also realized he used the late-night visits to do things she did not like. Initially, they proceeded to the kitchen where they chatted. While hanging out in the kitchen area, JonBenét consumed pineapple. After spending some time in the kitchen area, the perpetrator escorted JonBenét to the basement with an innocent guise of some sort. Though JonBenét saw through the ploy, she went anyway out of obligation.

Most likely, the two of them proceeded to the area just outside the wine cellar. The room is fairly secluded and it was carpeted. The perpetrator forced JonBenét into some kind of sexual game/act out of curiosity or possibly some deviant sexual gratification. The sexual games have been escalating in intensity during their recent encounters. This time the perpetrator puts a rope around JonBenét's neck.

He also uses a broken piece of a paint brush as a means to control the tightness of the rope. JonBenét was completely helpless, and she does not struggle because she believes it will be over shortly. As she is lying on her stomach, the perpetrator tightens and loosens the rope around her neck experimenting with the effects. The perpetrator has no experience using a rope and garrote in this manner, but utilizes them out of curiosity.

At some point, JonBenét, unaware of her impending unconsciousness, drifted away. She passed out. The strangulation was severe enough to kill her. In the eyes of the perpetrator, she appeared dead. The perpetrator was completely horrified! He did not mean for this to happen. He did not want to hurt her. He shook her, trying to awaken her from what he hoped was just a bout of unconsciousness. As he failed to pull her out of her slump, he panicked! He screamed at her to wake up! *This may be the screaming reportedly heard between midnight and 2:00 a.m.* He continued to shake her. As he was running out of ideas, he tried one final act that he hoped would pull her out of her unconsciousness. He struck her in the head with a blunt object, possibly a baseball bat, while crying out for her to wake up! His rage and fear regarding what had happened caused him to strike her with all of his force though it was not his intention. With that fatal blow, she ceased.

As the realization of the events began to sink in, the perpetrator was at a loss for what to do next. With almost no options left and an inability to handle it himself, he was left with no choice. He had to wake up Patsy Ramsey. He ascended the stairs from the basement all the way to the third floor. He slowly climbed the last set of stairs trying not to make any unnecessary noise. He went over to Patsy's side of the bed and gently woke her. He told her something was wrong with JonBenét. Patsy awoke in a confused and slightly disoriented state. John Ramsey did not awake when the individual woke up Patsy. He had taken a Melatonin the night before to help him sleep. In addition, according to Patsy's April 1997 official interviews, John was a deep sleeper.

Patsy and the individual started their descent toward the basement. Patsy asked the individual, "What happened?" over and over. She received responses of "I don't know," and "I think she might be sick or hurt." As they reached the area outside of the wine cellar, Patsy saw her baby lying on the floor, hopefully just resting. As she rushed to her, she quickly realized she was dead. JonBenét had a rope around her neck and wrists. Her pajama bottoms were pulled down. Patsy knew immediately it was not an accident in the traditional sense of the word. Her pleas and inquires with the perpetrator left her with no more information. The perpetrator's half denials and claims of ignorance fell on deaf ears. Patsy realized there was some level of culpability with the perpetrator, even if it was a quasi-accident or someone else was involved. However, her main focus at this point was saving JonBenét, which she quickly realized was futile.

Once the full gravity of the situation washed over Pasty, she realized she could not save her baby. And she also realized that someone else she dearly loved was involved in the death of her daughter. As a result, she faced the most horrific dilemma of her life. With nothing left to do to help JonBenét, Patsy made the fateful decision to protect the person she loved. She had to cover for him. Patsy had to gain her composure somehow. She sent the person away and began her scheming.

A plan would need to be developed to cast suspicion away from those close to JonBenét. There would have to be the appearance of an intruder. The body would need to be hidden and a motive devised. Patsy tried to carry JonBenét into the wine cellar to conceal her body. She was so heavy. Patsy had to drag her into the room by her arms. As a result, she pulled her arms over her head as she dragged her into the wine cellar. Because of the rigor mortis, JonBenét's arms stayed above her head after Patsy moved her.

JonBenét had abrasions on the back of her right shoulder, lower left back, and back of her left leg. The abrasions appeared rust colored. When Patsy dragged JonBenét into the wine cellar she caused the scratches to the rear of her body as she pulled her along the floor. The abrasions had a different appearance than normal scratches because they occurred post mortem.

Patsy placed duct tape over her mouth in an attempt to convey that she had to be silenced as she was taken from her room. Patsy found the roll of tape in the basement. After using the duct tape, she had to hide the roll because she wanted the crime to point toward an intruder. However, her plan was not for the police to find JonBenét's body. In one of many perplexing elements of this crime, the police never found the roll of duct tape. It is unlikely Patsy ever left the house on the night of December 25th; therefore, the tape was likely somewhere in the house. It is quite possible the police missed the roll of duct tape, but more likely, the duct tape was removed prior to the thorough searches.

Part of the reason behind why Patsy moved JonBenét's body was to conceal it. Patsy realized she would need to remove the body from the house in order to fully protect the perpetrator. She did not feel she could remove the body nor did she have the time to do so in the middle of the night. Her plan had to establish a viable opportunity to remove the body.

After she moved JonBenét into the wine cellar, Patsy executed the second and probably the most critical phase of her cover-up. She wrote the ransom note. Patsy went to the kitchen on the first floor. She sat down at the kitchen table and after much deliberation she crafted the ransom note with her left-hand. She started out by assigning blame to a foreign faction and supporting the claim by misspelling two words early in the note. She then requested an odd amount of $118,000, most likely a figure from her subconscious due to John's bonus earlier in the year.

The second component of the ransom note was the not-so-subtle requirement/instruction that John must *go to the bank*. Several lines discussed John actually physically going to the bank. John must leave the house in order for Patsy to get JonBenét out of the house. There is absolutely no indication Patsy had any kind of detailed plan or even a viable means for removing the body from the house. Nevertheless, she based a key part of her plan on having time to remove JonBenét from the house.

The third portion of the ransom note was designed to keep John from calling the police. Most people believe this is traditional ransom note language, and it is. However, Patsy's plan was very much predicated on John not contacting the police or anyone for that matter. Patsy needed to be left alone in the house so she could remove the body. The harsh tone in the note was a desperate attempt by Patsy to prevent John from calling the police. Patsy knew how much he loved his daughter so she believed that he would follow the note's directions for the sake of JonBenét. Nearing the end of that segment, she explicitly told John "not to grow a brain." She did not want him overthinking the situation. She just wanted him out of the house so she could complete the cover-up.

On the morning of December 26th around 5:45 a.m. John first read the ransom note. After a quick review, he told Patsy to call the police. Patsy was hesitant to call the police. She responded, "Are you sure?" (Ramsey 2001) Why did she hesitate? The implication was that the ransom note said not to call the police. However, Patsy claimed she had not read the entire note so would not have known that. Of course, she knew what the note said. Patsy did not want to call the police because that would prevent her from removing the body from the house; and thus, completing her cover-up. Other than referring to the threats in the note, Patsy did not have a good reason to not call the police as John instructed.

After completing the ransom note, she returned to the basement. She tucked JonBenét's white blanket around her to increase her warmth and comfort, even in death. After caring for her daughter, Patsy picked up an aluminum baseball bat and carried it to the first floor. She opened the butler door and dropped the bat on the back/side patio. This is possibly the metal scraping sound a neighbor claimed to have heard during the night. She left the butler door unlocked to demonstrate an intruder left through that door, throwing the bat as he left. The incompetence of the police response wrecked this portion of her plan. They did not identify the unlocked door or categorize it as a possible entrance/exit point for an intruder.

Once the door and baseball bat were staged, Patsy returned to the kitchen to get the ransom note. It is likely Patsy wore gloves while handling and writing the ransom note, but the police failed to recover any gloves or find any fingerprints. She placed the note at the base of the spiral staircase leading to the second floor. Most likely, the note was spread out, but not enough to cover the stair, as most tests found it nearly impossible to step over the note while descending the steps. Patsy then walked up the stairs and returned to bed. She slept only a few moments, if at all, as she waited for the next day to come and her plan to unfold. She knew there was nothing she could have done to save JonBenét. Once Patsy called the police, she realized her plan was compromised. The outcome of the previous night's events would be determined by circumstances primarily out of her control.

If the police had gotten to interrogate Patsy prior to legal involvement, it is likely they would have been able to determine some of what went on that fateful night. Patsy was an emotional wreck, and it is unlikely she would have maintained a consistent story. She would have provided detectives with the details necessary to unravel what transpired.

Unfortunately, the police did not insist on thoroughly interviewing the Ramseys on December 26th.

The Ramsey's lawyers successfully kept John and Patsy out of prison. It was most likely worth it to Patsy. However, John was innocent. He was only guilty of blindness toward the events on the night of December 25th. The decision to avoid the police and endure the onslaught by the media could not have been worth it to John Ramsey. He believed everyone in his family was innocent. If he truly believed in everyone's innocence, coming clean early on would have alleviated much of the extreme stress they endured during the first couple of years of the investigation. In the end, the truth died with Patsy Ramsey. She did not turn on the person she loved dearly.

In the Ramsey's book, *The Death of Innocence*, Patsy Ramsey wrote the following:

> In a strange and unexpected way, I had unconsciously woven death into the fabric of our Christmas celebration, and, of course, couldn't have imagined in my wildest nightmare how that 1996 Christmas season would end for us. I couldn't help but feel that there had been a premonition in my

selecting purple ribbon for our Christmas tree. Without an awareness of its significance, I had place [sic] the meaning of Lent in the midst of our celebration of the nativity.

There are many ways to interpret this excerpt and most are not favorable to Patsy's innocence. Though, one could argue she was merely exhibiting guilt over not protecting her child. It would be expected that a parent of a murdered child would have tremendous guilt. However, the above statement does not convey guilt at all. Patsy also indicated she had a "premonition."

What did Patsy witness or experience prior to Christmas 1996 that would lead her to believe something of this nature was to occur, even if it was on a subconscious level? Since Patsy knew something terrible would happen, it indicates, at some level, she was aware of circumstances or signs not obvious to those around her. Patsy's expression of her premonition indicates it was someone close to her who was most likely involved in JonBenét's demise. How else would she have had the inputs that drove her premonition?

Patsy elaborated by stating she placed the meaning of Lent into their holiday celebration. What did she mean with this comment? Lent means different things to different people and it varies among cultures. In general, Lent is seen as a time to purify by weaning from sin through self-denial. From what activities did Patsy have to wean herself that had to do with the death of JonBenét? What desires and temptations did she have to forgo? It is an eerie thought. She most likely viewed her daughter's death as the end of Lent; and as a result, the time prior to the incident became Lent in retrospect. However, with the numerous accusations floating around JonBenét's death at the time of the Ramsey's publication, the entire segment presented a creepy and dark tone around Patsy's thoughts and feelings about what happened.

In response to a question from Barbara Walters, Patsy stated: "…If I have a regret it's I didn't get more help…that morning." Patsy had a premonition this was going to happen to JonBenét, and her biggest regret is she did not do more to help? Most likely, Patsy is referring to the morning prior to finding the note when she was concealing what happened to JonBenét. She wished that she could have gotten to her daughter sooner so that she could have gotten her more help. Otherwise, her assistance after she found the note would not have made any difference in the life of her daughter.

As Patsy Ramsey accurately stated during a press conference: "We feel like there are at least two people on the face of this earth that know who did this. And that is the killer, and someone that that person may have confided in." Patsy was the individual he told and the person responsible for JonBenét's death falls within a very narrow category. It was a person Patsy loved and cared for so deeply she would risk her own welfare to protect. Patsy would lie about the death of her beloved daughter in order to protect this individual. She did not act to cover-up the events of December 25, 1996 to protect herself or her husband. It is someone else.

There will never be a conviction involving the death of JonBenét. The incompetence of those in charge in Boulder destroyed the case. The only hope for closure is to find out the truth. Many questions have been answered, but many still remain.

Works Cited

Auge, Karen. "Evidence voluminous but tricky." Denver Post. 1999.

Bardsley, Marilyn, and Patrick Bellamy. "Murder of JonBenét Ramsey." *truTV*, date unknown.

Bunker, M.N. Handwriting Analysis: The Science of Determining Personality by Graphoanalysis. Chicago, IL, 1979.

Daly, D.J., C. Murphy and S.D. McDermott. "The transfer of touch DNA from hands to glass, fabric and wood." *Forensic Science International: Genetics*, January, 2012.

Gentile, Don, ed., and David Wright, ed. JonBenét - The Police Files. Boca Raton, FL, 2003.

Hodges, Andrew G. A Mother gone Bad. Birmingham, AL, 1998.

Kolar, James A. Foreign Faction. Telluride, CO, 2012.

Leung, Rebecca."JonBenét: DNA Rules Out Parents." CBSNews.com. February 11, 2009.

Maloney, J.J., and J. Patrick O'Connor."The Murder of JonBenét Ramsey." *Crime Magazine*, May 7, 1999.

McClish, Mark. I Know You Are Lying; Detecting Deception Through Statement Analysis. Winterville, NC, 2001.

McClish, Mark. "JonBenét Ramsey Ransom Note – Part I." Statement Analysis, July 9, 2001.

McDonough, Sam Dennis. 120 Clues That Show Who Killed JonBenét. August 4, 2011.

Ramsey, John and Patsy. The Death of Innocence. New York, 2001.

Shiller, Lawrence. Perfect Murder, Perfect Town. New York, 1999.

Taleb, Nassim, The Black Swan: The Impact of the Highly Improbable. April 17, 2007.

Thomas, Steve, and Don Davis. JonBenét – Inside the Ramsey Murder Investigation. New York, NY, 2000.

Unknown Author. "The Clue that Breaks the Case." Shadowgov.com, date unknown.

Wecht, Cyril, and Charles Bosworth, Jr. Who Killed JonBenét Ramsey? Harmondsworth, Middlesex, England, 1998.

Interviews

Burden of Proof, April 28, 2000, with Greta Van Susteren and Roger Cossack

Burden of Proof, August 29, 2000, with Greta Van Susteren and Roger Cossack

CNN, January 1, 1997, with Brian Cabell

The Geraldo Rivera Show, February 27, 1997, with Geraldo Rivera

Larry King Live, March 4, 1997, with Wolf Blitzer

Larry King Live, March 27-28, 2000, with Larry King

Larry King Live, May 31, 2000, with Larry King

Peter Boyles Radio Show, July 21, 1998, with Peter Boyles

Today Show, March 20-24, 2000, with Katie Couric

20/20, March 15, 2000, with Barbara Walters

48 Hours, October 4, 2002, with Erin Moriarty

Other References

A Candy Rose Timeline, www.acandyrose.com, "The Bonita Papers," 1999, accessed September 2011 – October 2011.

"Flight 755 15th Street, Passengers in the Vortex," www.acandyrose.com, accessed September, 2011.

JonBenét Case Encyclopedia, www.jonbenetramsey.pbworks.com, accessed September 2011 – October 2011.

Websleuths.com, accessed September, 2011.

3123599R00154

Printed in Great Britain
by Amazon.co.uk, Ltd.,
Marston Gate.